W9-ANX-144

Dealing with comparison is easy as long as you don't own a phone, use the internet, or ever leave the house. If you, like me, do any of those things, though, you're going to need Nona's new book. To get to the heart of who you are and the root of comparison, read this!

JON ACUFF, *New York Times* bestselling author of
Soundtracks: The Surprising Solution to Overthinking

This book is all things Nona Jones—strength, individuality, and daring vulnerability wrapped up in one amazing message glorifying Christ! From the first page, *Killing Comparison* takes you on a journey from feeling insecure over your differences to truly feeling valued for the very same reasons.

SADIE ROBERTSON HUFF, author, speaker, and founder of Live Original

In her masterful work *Killing Comparison*, Nona Jones exposes and addresses one of the major contributors to people failing to experience their best life and become their best self: comparison. This work is timely, necessary, and destined to set people free.

DR. DHARIUS DANIELS, lead pastor of Change Church, author
of *Relational Intelligence* and *Your Purpose Is Calling*

In a world that seems determined to make us believe we aren't good enough comes *Killing Comparison*. Nona Jones has taken a well-known Bible story and turned it on its head to help us see with new eyes how to get free from comparison-born insecurity. This is a message everyone needs to read.

CAREY NIEUWHOF, bestselling author, podcaster, and
founder of the Art of Leadership Academy

Whether you are a single woman, corporate executive, Sunday school teacher, or high school student, you need the message of *Killing Comparison*. Nona Jones has stripped insecurity down to its core to help us see it for what it is and get free from its toxic grip on our hearts.

DR. ANITA PHILLIPS, LCSW-C, trauma therapist,
host of the *In the Light* podcast

Ever have the gnawing feeling that you just don't measure up? Well, fear no longer. Nona Jones, in *Killing Comparison*, kills the notion that you aren't good enough. Nona tackles negative self-talk and the external forces that attempt to put a lid on the potential inside you. A must-read!

DR. A. R. BERNARD, founder and senior pastor of the Christian Cultural Center, author of *Four Things Women Want from a Man*

Killing Comparison is the book we all need to read to stay grounded in the truth about our identity. It's easy to believe the lie that we don't measure up when every magazine article and social media post seems to focus on our deficiencies. But Nona Jones lovingly reminds us that "even what we lack has purpose."

ANTHONY O'NEAL, #1 *Wall Street Journal* bestselling author and speaker

KILLING

comparison

KILLING
comparison

Reject the Lie You
Aren't Good Enough
and Live Confident in Who
God Made You to Be

NONA JONES

ZONDERVAN
BOOKS

ZONDERVAN BOOKS

Killing Comparison
Copyright © 2022 by Nona Jones

Requests for information should be addressed to:
Zondervan, *3900 Sparks Dr. SE, Grand Rapids, Michigan 49546*

Zondervan titles may be purchased in bulk for educational, business, fundraising, or sales promotional use. For information, please email SpecialMarkets@Zondervan.com.

ISBN 978-0-310-36523-5 (hardcover)
ISBN 978-0-310-36525-9 (audio)
ISBN 978-0-310-36524-2 (ebook)

Cover design: Curt Diepenhorst
Cover photo: James Schlefstein, www.hidefpixel.com
Interior design: Sara Colley

Printed in the United States of America

22 23 24 25 26 27 28 29 30 31 32 /LSC/ 15 14 13 12 11 10 9 8 7 6 5 4 3 2 1

To everyone who has ever felt like you were less-than because it seemed like someone else was more.

CONTENTS

PART 4: FINAL THOUGHTS

AN INVITATION TO KILL COMPARISON

If you're anything like me, you have probably read several books about insecurity. To grapple with my own issues, I have read books by incredibly thoughtful and wise authors; some are well-known Bible teachers and others are well-respected therapists. But as insightful as I found many of those books to be, the reason I wrote this book is because some of those books felt clinical. They felt detached. They felt more like theological medicine than a personal journey toward healing from insecurity.

Therefore, when I decided to write this book, I chose to provide my personal, honest, unfiltered journey, something that requires a level of vulnerability that makes my heart palpitate. No, really; with every keystroke I found my heart racing because I had to put on display some feelings and imperfections that I would prefer to keep hidden. My biggest fear, in full transparency, was that someone would read this and think, "Whew, she's a mess. Why would anyone ever listen to her?" But I've laid myself bare on these pages because your freedom is worth the cost of my pride.

I want you to know you are not alone. I want you to know you are not broken. I want you to know you hold my heart in your hands because you hold my truth in your hands. But it isn't my truth alone. It is *ours*. My hope is that, after you read this book, you will experience the true and lasting peace that comes only from killing the toxic comparison that so desperately wants to destroy your sense of identity and worth. My prayer is that you will stand boldly and confidently in the truth that nothing you *do* can make you more worthy than simply being who you *are* in Jesus. Let's get started.

"Let the one who boasts boast in the Lord." For it is not the one who commends himself who is approved, but the one whom the Lord commends. (2 Corinthians 10:17–18)

Part One

THE LIES THEY TOLD ME

Chapter One

EVERYONE IS INVITED
. . . EXCEPT YOU

I leaped out of bed when the alarm signaled it was time to wake up and hit the pavement. Ten minutes later, I was outside pressing "start running" on my fitness app and putting in my earbuds to listen to a worship music playlist. I was excited to run because the cool, crisp mornings between winter and spring are my favorite time of year. Although the April sky was still dark, threads of orange and purple streaked across it as the sun rose. My heart was light and joyful despite the unsettling times we had all been recently thrust into as the pandemic brought the world to a screeching halt.

Around mile four I began a conversation with God. I thanked him for my life, family, work, ministry, friendships, and the gift of healthy lungs that allow me to run. I prayed for wisdom to carry me and my team through an unknown future—one that required helping churches around the world figure out how to operate without gathering in a building. As the head of global faith partnerships at Facebook, I had received more calls, texts, emails, and direct messages from pastors and church leaders during the first weeks of COVID-19 than I had in the three years prior.

As I reached mile six, a favorite song came on, and I did a run-dance on the sidewalk as drivers-by looked at me in confusion. I punched the air and clapped with the beat while singing, "Trust in the Lord with all your heart! Trust in the Lord with all your mind! Trust in the Lord with all your strength! Lean not on your own understanding!" The upbeat tempo always got me pumped, but I had no idea that an hour later my trust in the Lord would be put to the test.

I made it home just in time to give my seven- and ten-year-old sons sweaty hugs and my husband a sweaty kiss before they left for the day. Then I started my post-run routine of showering, stretching, making a pot of tea, and having some quiet time with the Lord. I was looking forward to my Bible study time because the cancelation of many of my speaking engagements allowed me to study for the fun of it without the pressure of preparing to give a message.

The Holy Spirit had led me to take an interest in the life of Jonathan, King Saul's son. A lot was written about his father, and even more was written about his best friend, David, but I had never looked closely at Jonathan. I started reading in 1 Samuel 14, which tells the story of how Jonathan waged an attack on a Philistine outpost with only his young armor-bearer by his side. As Jonathan made his way to Mikmash to fight two dozen Philistines by himself, his father, the king, rested comfortably under a pomegranate tree in Gibeah with six hundred soldiers. The juxtaposition of the two scenes was striking.

When Jonathan and his young armor-bearer reached the outpost, they saw that the Philistines were positioned on a cliff. This put Jonathan and his armor-bearer at a strategic disadvantage because it robbed them of the element of surprise. The climb to the Philistines' position would also use precious energy they needed for the battle. Nevertheless, Jonathan turned to his armor-bearer and said, "Come, let's go over to the outpost of those uncircumcised men. Perhaps the LORD will act in our behalf. Nothing can hinder the LORD from saving, whether by many or by few" (1 Samuel 14:6).

I repeated that last line to myself: "Nothing can hinder the Lord from saving, whether by many or by few." Something about it resonated. *When the Lord is for us, we can be outnumbered but are never unprotected.*

I read a couple more chapters and then decided it was time to start my day. I quickly checked my Facebook page to respond to comments and messages and then did the same on Instagram. Although I normally go straight to my Instagram notifications, that day I caught a glimpse of my newsfeed first. And that's when the downward emotional spiral started.

> When the Lord is for us, we can be outnumbered but are never unprotected.

FRIEND 1: Hey, friends! I'm so excited to announce that I'm joining the speaker lineup for Susie Sacred's Full Blossom Conference. Visit the link in my bio to register, and meet me online next month with an incredible roster of speakers!

> **FRIEND 2:** I'm beyond ecstatic to share that I'll be speaking at the Full Blossom Conference next month with Susie Sacred and an amazing roster of the best speakers across every sector. Will you be there? Comment below to let me know!
>
> **FRIEND 3:** Next month is going to be epic! Join me and other amazing speakers at the Full Blossom Conference with Susie Sacred online next month. I have a message for *you*. Tag a friend and register at fullblossom.com!

After scrolling for what felt like an eternity, I counted no fewer than eight friends posting the exciting news that they were joining an amazing roster of speakers for a major women's conference that was going virtual because of the pandemic. Since I don't follow many people on social media, it seemed like the only thing in my newsfeed was an avalanche of exciting announcements about speaking at the Full Blossom Conference.

"Why wasn't *I* invited to speak?" I asked aloud. "It's like Susie asked everyone we mutually know except me."

With each new post, I felt what can only be described as the stab of an emotional ice pick to the heart. My mind was clouded with hurt, so I stopped scrolling, closed Instagram, and looked out my living room window into a beautiful day. The skies were blue and filled with fluffy white clouds. Birds bounded from limb to limb on the tree just outside my window. But the beauty outside couldn't overcome the ugliness churning inside me.

I was scheduled to join a video conference, but I was so distracted by confusion and pain that I went to the kitchen to make another pot of tea. As I stirred the honey into my teacup and watched the golden sweetness dissolve into the hot water, I was flooded with "why" questions.

Why was I left out?
Why was I not considered?
Why was I overlooked?
Why was I not worthy of an invitation?

An old, familiar hurt resurfaced inside—the hurt of being unwanted.

I've had a full speaking schedule for years, despite never once advertising myself as a speaker or asking to speak at events. And I receive more speaking invitations for business and church conferences than I can accept. I've been invited to speak on multiple continents and keynoted major conferences across the United States and abroad. Yet, somehow, not being invited to speak at *this* conference bothered me.

I'd heard of Full Blossom before and had never desired to speak at it, but after I saw many of the people in my ministry circle invited to speak there, my exclusion catalyzed a self-worth inquisition. Comparison makes what never mattered before the thing that matters most.

As I sat down at my desk and opened my laptop, I felt a magnetic pull back to Instagram. I had back-to-back video conferences every thirty minutes for the next seven hours, so I set my phone down and logged on for the first meeting. Within ten minutes, I had discreetly unlocked my phone, opened Instagram, and continued the scroll. An irresistible and poisonous thread tugged on my heart and distracted me from work.

I went to Susie's profile and saw post after post of her gushing about each speaker: how incredible they were and how perfect the conference would be because of them. My chest tightened, and a lump grew in my throat as I watched a video of her enthusiastically naming several of my friends as speakers. Although she spoke about them, my heart heard her speaking to me: *Nona, I know who you are. I've seen what you do. And you're not good enough. You're not what I'm looking for. You're just average.*

I had not only constructed the full-blown, play-by-play narrative for why Susie hadn't invited me but also decided I needed to unfollow everyone she had invited to speak. My heart felt like it would shatter if I saw one more friend's post about the awesome conference I wasn't invited to speak at. I didn't want to wade through endless reminders that they were speaking at the conference and I wasn't.

"Why did she pick everyone around me but not me?" I asked aloud again. The more I thought about it, the more my hurt turned to anger. But in my anger, I heard the Holy Spirit ask a different question: "Why does it matter?"

"Why does it matter?" I responded incredulously. "Because everyone who's anyone will be speaking there. And I'm not. This will be the largest online women's ministry gathering of the year, and I will be absent."

"So you think you matter only because of the speaking invitations you receive?" the Holy Spirit asked.

"No," I said. "I know I matter to *you*. I just . . . I just . . ." I stammered as the weight of the truth settled on me.

"Go ahead," the Holy Spirit prompted, "say it."

"I just want to matter to *them* too," I whispered, tears forming in the corners of my eyes.

"I know, Nona. You want to matter to them because you're insecure," the Holy Spirit said matter-of-factly.

"Insecure?" I responded with disbelief. "I'm not insecure! Far from it. I know who I am in you. I preach about it regularly. Besides, I have everything I could ever want and more than I could ever have imagined. I'm definitely *not* insecure!"

With love and conviction, the Holy Spirit said, "Nona, you think people are insecure if they don't like how they look or don't like what they have or don't like what they do. Those are *expressions* of insecurity, but they're not the *root* of insecurity. The root of insecurity is when your identity is built on an insecure foundation."

As I considered what the Holy Spirit said, I felt defensive. "My identity is secured to you, Lord. I know what the Word says about who I am, and I believe it. How can you say I'm insecure?"

"Yes, you know what my Word says, and you also believe it," affirmed the Holy Spirit. "But knowledge and belief are not the same as faith. As long as you know my Word in your head and believe it in your heart but don't practice it daily, your identity will continue to be secured to the affirmation of others. You have built your identity on people's approval. People show their approval with likes on social media, but I demonstrated my approval through love on the cross. I approved of you before you were formed in your mother's womb. And my approval is unchanging."

The truth in these words hit me like a Mack truck. So much of my life had been spent trying to win people's approval, and maybe yours has too:

- That time in high school when you were one of the "it" girls and got invited to all the best parties and hangouts—until

THE LIES THEY TOLD ME

you were no longer invited. A wealthy new girl started attending the school and your friends decided there wasn't enough room in the clique for both of you, so they kicked you out to make room for her.

- Those months when your calendar was filled with business travel and making deals on multiple continents while wining and dining with the powerful—until, without explanation, your calls started going to voicemail and your emails went unreturned. A new company emerged on the scene, and everyone wanted to do deals with them instead.

- Those years when you were your pastor's favorite Sunday school teacher and he placed you in charge of the entire Sunday school department—until he decided your style was outdated and brought in a skinny-jeans-wearing kid with a mohawk and a TikTok following to "get things back on track."

The approval of others is never permanent, and it often depends on variables that are beyond our control. People use things such as height, weight, wealth, popularity, theology, position, or political affiliation as "approval filters" to determine whether we're good enough for them. Yet God approved of us before there was anything to approve of. God created us *on* purpose, *with* purpose.

> God created us *on* purpose, *with* purpose.

The Holy Spirit said, "Nona, the reason you're hurt by not being invited to speak at that conference is because you measure your worth based on how much people approve of you *compared* to others. When you aren't secured to the stable foundation of who *I* say you are, you drift with the shifting currents of others' opinions about you. When you drift from me, you have to secure your identity to people's opinions to stay afloat. Your insecurity didn't start this morning. You've been insecure most of your life."

I sat in silence with my eyes closed, reflecting on what the Holy Spirit had said. Before I knew it, my eyes were brimming with tears. The Holy Spirit was right—as always.

Somewhere along the line, I had surrendered my purpose for performative applause. God had valued me before I even had the ability to perform my way into his love. Though God determined I was worth dying for at my worst (Romans 5:8), I made the mistake of conflating my eternal, intrinsic value with likes, follows, shares, and speaking invitations. And the craziest part of it all is that no one knew. *Not even me.* It happened subtly, over time.

With every larger platform I stepped onto, my heart had slowly detached from the secure foundation of God's approval and attached itself to the insecure foundation of other people's approval, creating insecurity.

"Lord, you're right," I said. "You say in your Word that people honor you with their lips but their hearts are far from you. I now understand what you mean. I have honored you with my lips, but I'm not honoring you with my life. Lord, I need your help. Please deliver me from insecurity."

"Nona, what you're asking will require more than you expect, but if you trust me and obey me, I will help you get to freedom. You must no longer look to others for approval; you must look only to me."

"Lord, I'm ready," I said.

"No, you're not. But that's what my grace is for."

Just as Jonathan was outnumbered against the Philistines, we can feel overwhelmed by seeming to never measure up. But the same divine grace that enabled *his* victory is the same grace that enables our victory over insecurity too.

Making Sense of Comparison

I'm guessing you're no stranger to the lure of comparison. Maybe you just found out your best friend is getting married. Even though you're devastated, you put on a fake smile, embrace her with warm hugs, and offer to host her bridal shower. You thought you would be the first to get married, but the man of your dreams told you he didn't love you anymore and decided your cousin was a better fit for his future.

Or perhaps you've been working your butt off for a promotion, but instead of hearing, "Congratulations, you got the job," you heard, "We've decided to go with an external candidate." You did everything your manager said you needed to do to prepare for the opportunity, but when it came down to it, the job went to someone who had never sacrificed anything for the company.

Maybe you just found out your college roommate, who never cared about politics in college, was elected to the United States Congress on their first attempt, while you, who have lived and breathed politics since serving as a class president in middle school, have multiple failed campaigns to your credit.

When others achieve something that we desperately wanted or worked for, a painful question inevitably arises: Why them, not me?

- Why didn't my boyfriend propose to me after I gave him the best years of my life, but Scott proposed to Sarah after just six months?
- Why is this outsider going to be my boss when I'm the one who has kept the team moving forward and am just as qualified for the position?
- Why have my efforts to get elected to local and state offices been soul-crushing failures, but my college roommate's first run for Congress was a wild success?

All these questions can be reduced to one root question: Why am I not good enough *compared to them*?

This question has haunted me every time someone else has received an opportunity that I had my heart set on. I would mentally stack up my credentials next to theirs to figure out how I fell short. Insecurity uses other people as the measuring stick for our worth. When the opportunity I wanted went to someone who had more experience or notoriety than I did, the pill was still bitter, but *at least* I could make sense of it. It was much harder to make sense of why an opportunity went to someone else if I couldn't identify how I had fallen short. How could I make sense of not being chosen "just because"?

When I compared my qualifications and social media reach with those of several of the others who were chosen to speak at the Full Blossom Conference, I struggled to make sense of why I had been left out. I couldn't identify meaningful differences between them and me, and in several cases, I had more experience and more social media followers. Then I considered another variable: Did the speakers have a closer relationship with Susie than I did? She and I weren't super close, so maybe the others were closer to her than I was. As I did my comparison-fueled sleuthing work, including texting a few friends to ask how they knew Susie, I found out that she didn't even know several of the people she'd invited. So why them and not me?

Once again, the Holy Spirit asked me, "Why does it matter, Nona?" I didn't have a good answer.

But it *definitely* mattered.

It mattered so much that I scoured the speakers' Instagram profiles and Facebook pages to calculate their reach and engagement *in comparison to my own*.

It mattered so much that I visited their websites and reviewed their upcoming events to see how many major conferences they were headlining *in comparison to me*.

It mattered so much that I checked their lists of followers to see how many celebrities and media organizations were following them *in comparison to me*.

Although in retrospect I know I was being childish, if you're anything like me, you've probably never asked yourself "why does it matter" when drowning in feelings of inadequacy. You simply did what I did; launched into a Jacques Cousteau–level exploration of the depth of another person's beauty, wealth, or influence to calculate how you measure up *in comparison to them*. But we can't compare perfection to perfection. Allow me to explain.

French Impressionist artist Edgar Degas once said, "Painting is easy when you don't know how, but very difficult when you do."[1] In other words, amateur artists can paint with a level of irreverence that allows them to present even what might be seen as sloppy work with pride. But master artists pick up the tools of their artistry with a high degree of respect for their craft and their creation. And no work of art is considered finished until it reaches perfection in their eyes. For this reason, a true master artist would never compare one work of art with another work of art because they are *both* perfect in their eyes.

We tend to think perfection is in the eye of the *beholder*, but no. Perfection is not in the eye of the beholder; perfection is in the eye of the *creator*. It is for this reason that comparing a priceless work of art with another priceless work is impossible for the creator—*but simple for those beholding the creation.*

Imagine being a handmade porcelain vase sitting in a display cabinet next to other porcelain vases. You and the other vases are all available for purchase, but the display has four rows of vases, and you're in the last row at the back of the cabinet. As you observe the vases near the front, you wonder what it is about them that merited more prominent placement. You take note of their size, shape, color, and unique artistic markings etched across their surfaces.

> Perfection is not in the eye of the beholder; perfection is in the eye of the *creator.*

"I'm shorter than that one and rounder than that other one," you observe. "That one is purple, but I'm green. And I don't have any artistic etchings." You conclude that these traits—the ones you don't have—must be what gave the other vases more prominent placement. Suddenly, the characteristics that made you perfect in your creator's eyes become the very ones that cause you to question your value. As you secure your sense of worth to what you don't have—based on comparison—you feel insecure. Shaky. Unstable.

Experienced potters often design their vases as sketches before they grab a lump of clay and form it on the pottery wheel.

They have a vision before they shape a vessel. The same principle applies to you. You began as a vision in the Potter's heart before you took shape in his hands. Your unique value and identity were skillfully designed before you were formed. This is why it's unwise to compare yourself with anyone else. The divine Potter designs every person with a unique purpose according to his own vision of perfection, so why would we try to compare our own perfection with someone else's perfection? Let me tell you why.

Right now I have almost seventy thousand followers on Instagram. Given that the average person has 150 followers, my follower count places me in the top 5 percent of Instagram accounts. But before we throw a celebration, I should also point out a couple more people who have far more followers than I do. For example, Dwayne "The Rock" Johnson has 298 million followers. That's 60 million *more* than Beyoncé. (I know, right? How?) While my account is considered a "top account," it would be crazy to compare myself to The Rock or Beyoncé.

Since I know competing with people who are at the level of Beyoncé and The Rock would be impossible, toxic comparison causes me to dismiss what is unattainable and to set my sights lower. Toxic comparison leads me to set my sights on a person who is ever so slightly beyond my grasp but still within my reach if I just work a little harder. A person I *should* be able to be as good as or even better than if I simply put in a little effort.

When we suffer from toxic comparison, we identify people in our social circle who have an attainable degree of success. Once we have them in our line of sight, we secure our identity (often unknowingly) to getting to where they are on the worthiness ruler. Our goal is to get to where they are on that measuring stick. But every time they advance further ahead—with a new relationship, promotion, pound lost, or major speaking engagement—our identity feels threatened because their success moves them further out of reach. We have made them our standard for perfection without understanding that we are perfect beyond compare to our Creator.

Pegging our identity and self-worth to the people we believe we should be as good as, if not better than, is so deeply embedded in our human nature that we don't even realize we're doing it—until we find ourselves sitting in our office with our camera off during a video conference because we're snot-bubble crying after being left out of a conference we had never even desired to speak at.

Exposing Insecurity

If you're tired of feeling that emotional ice pick stab your heart every time [insert name] achieves something new, I invite you to join me on a journey toward freedom and healing. It won't be an easy journey, but it will be worth it. I believe God is calling you to secure your identity to the only true and unwavering foundation: who your Creator made you to be and the unique purpose only you can fulfill.

Although social media often gets blamed for causing insecurity, I believe the truth is far more complicated. We didn't wake up one day after scrolling through Twitter, Snapchat, Instagram, or Facebook and suddenly question our worth. Instead, many of us come to those platforms with a self-worth that is tenuous to begin with. There is a root problem that existed before social media, and this is the problem we need to excavate and repair.

Instead of social media causing insecurity, I believe we bring our insecurities to social media. Why? Because we can have everything social media promises and still be insecure.

We can have material possessions and not have joy.

We can have the perfect Instagram gallery and not have peace.

We can have a marriage others envy and not have fulfillment.

Every time comparison makes you ask why—"Why was I left out? Why was I overlooked?"—ask yourself instead, "Why does it matter?"

Asking this question is important because experiences that *expose* your insecurity are not the *source* of your insecurity. In other words, someone else's material possessions, appearance, or perfect relationship is not the source of your insecurity. The source of your insecurity has a history, and you must explore that history to repair the soil of your heart and prepare it for healing and freedom.

Asking "Why does it matter?" has led to groundbreaking personal insight because it forces me to be honest about what I believe to be true and why. It forced me to get at the root of my insecurity by bringing me face-to-face with myself and interrupting the natural downward spiral into thoughts of inadequacy that usually accompanies a toxic comparison trigger. Now when I think I'm not good enough, pausing to consider those four words brings me back to myself.

As you begin this journey with me, my prayer is that each chapter will equip you to overcome comparison and to attach your identity to a secure foundation. To help you on your way, each chapter concludes with a four-piece toolbox:

RECALL lists the key teaching points from the chapter.

RECEIVE offers a guiding Scripture to contemplate.

RECITE provides a prayer you can pray based on the chapter theme.

REFLECT offers closing insights based on what healing has looked like in my own life.

I invite you to use this toolbox to pause and reflect. Then join me in the next chapter to explore how our past experiences reverberate through the present-day beliefs that shape us.

Recall

When the Lord is for us, we can be outnumbered but are never unprotected.

Why does it matter?

Insecurity uses other people as the measuring stick for our worth.

The root of insecurity is building your identity on an insecure foundation.

Comparison makes what never mattered before the thing that matters most.

God created us *on* purpose, *with* purpose.

Perfection is not in the eye of the beholder; perfection is in the eye of the creator.

You began as a vision in the Potter's heart before you took shape in his hands.

Experiences that *expose* your insecurity are not the *source* of your insecurity.

Receive

Trust in the LORD with all your heart
> and lean not on your own understanding;
in all your ways submit to him,
> and he will make your paths straight. (Proverbs 3:5–6)

Recite

Lord, help me to understand that I am more than the invitations I do or don't receive. I am more than the friendships I do or don't have. I am more than the things I think I can't live without because I believe they give me value. Help me to understand and believe in my heart that I have value because I am yours and because you made me perfect and unique.

Reflect

As I stewed in the pain I felt from being left out, God issued a challenge that knocked me off my feet. Susie and her team ended up having issues advertising their event on Facebook and Instagram and reached out to see if I could help. The petty version of me would have found a way to avoid responding to the email. Instead, I took the challenge and made sure my team helped them to get back up and running. Regardless of why I was left out, that God placed me in a position to help was its own form of blessing.

If that person who triggers toxic comparison in you comes to you for help, prayerfully consider whether God may be offering you a blessing—an opportunity to detoxify your system with the antivenom of kindness, mercy, and grace.

Chapter Two

NOBODY WANTS YOUR BODY

This chapter and the next recount traumatic events that may trigger painful memories in those who have survived physical, sexual, or verbal abuse. If you feel anxious while reading, feel free to skip to chapter 4.

I could hardly sleep from excitement. I was only a few weeks into my first year of high school, and I had saved my best outfit for this day. Most kids wear all their new clothes and shoes the first week of school, but I took a different approach, hoping to savor the good feelings I had every time I put on a new outfit. I wore a new outfit every few days, allowing me to extend my new wardrobe for weeks. And I always saved the best for last.

I got out of bed at my usual 5:40 a.m. and made myself a breakfast of eggs and corned beef hash. I mixed everything together in a bowl and then drowned it in ketchup. I poured a tall glass of juice and lathered some toast with butter and jelly.

After I cleaned my plate and downed my juice, I went back to my room to get ready for school. I excitedly ripped the tags from my flowy white blouse and jean skirt before putting them on. I pulled my new shoes out of their shoebox and slipped them on. Then I combed my hair and ran a lip gloss wand across my lips for the finishing touch. The girl staring back at me in the mirror was looking good. I grabbed my backpack and headed out the door to catch my bus.

"Are you coming to the football game tonight?" my friend Savannah asked as I walked into first-period Spanish class.

"No, I'm not really into sports," I answered.

"What! Football is everything here. You should come. You can hang out with me and my friends."

Savannah was a tenth grader and had taken a liking to me on my first day of school. She had an easygoing nature that was different from many of the other girls who always seemed anxious and perturbed for no obvious reason. Although she had friends, she wasn't cliquish; I never saw her exclude someone or try to make them feel like they were outside her friendship circle. She had introduced me to a few of her friends and made it a point to wave or say hi whenever our paths crossed. Given her insistence that I attend the game—and my secret desire to show off my outfit and hair—I decided to go.

A small group of us met in the courtyard after school and walked to the football field together. It was a hot, humid, and sticky Florida afternoon. The bleachers were fully exposed to the sun, making the heat almost unbearable, but being with Savannah and her friends helped distract me from the temperature. We passed the time by talking about everything from our favorite music to our favorite movies to our favorite clothing brands. When the conversation turned to how much everyone liked Bongo jeans, I had to admit I didn't own any.

"What!" said Savannah's friend Jennifer in surprise. She raised her auburn eyebrows high into her hairline and asked, "Why not?"

I shrugged my shoulders.

"Nona, you *have* to get some Bongos to be stylish!"

I didn't tell my new friends that the reason I didn't have any was because they didn't fit me. I had tried on several pairs of their largest size before the start of the school year. Although I had won the struggle to pull a pair of Bongo shorts over my extra thick thighs, when I forced the four buttons closed, my stomach spilled over the top of the shorts like a split can of biscuits. I'm pretty sure I broke several nails in the process.

As the sun descended on the horizon, the cheerleaders arrived and began their warm-up stretches. Their white uniforms were pristine, and they all wore their hair in ponytails accentuated by orange and green ribbons.

"I should try out," I thought.

I had been the captain of my middle school dance team, so I figured making the team wouldn't be too difficult. As they contorted themselves into splits and bounced up and down doing various toe touches, members of the band started arriving, and parents and students filled the bleachers. As the last few streaks of daylight waned across the sky, humongous floodlights illuminated the field with nighttime daylight. An announcer shouted over the public-address system, "Gooood evening, students, parents, friends, and guests! Game time starts in fifteen minutes, so grab your snacks and drinks, and get ready for some action!"

Savannah noticed a guy friend of hers with a group of his

friends and signaled them to sit with us. There was nowhere for them to sit because the space was crowded, but she shouted, "Nathan, come sit with us! We'll make room." He waved back, nodded, then motioned his friends toward where we sat.

As he made his way up the bleachers, I noticed he was cute. He was wearing an orange and green varsity jacket and fitted jeans. He was tall and had curly, dark brown hair, and shimmering hazel-green eyes. I had liked boys only from afar up until then and had never had a boyfriend. I immediately felt shy and tried not to stare.

To make room for him and his friends, we had to stand up and lean against the rail in front of us to let them pass by. Given how little space there was between the rail, our bench, and the people sitting in the row behind us, his friends had to do some gymnastics to get by. Although his friends made it without incident, as Nathan tried to squeeze behind me, he lost his balance and his pelvis rubbed against my butt.

"Agh!" I yelled in shock.

When he looked up and saw his friends laughing at him, his face turned red and he turned to me and said, "What are you screaming for? I don't want you! With a body like that, you're not good for anything but sex with the lights off, anyway."

His friends burst out laughing and said, "Ooohhh!"

My heart shattered.

"Nona, don't pay him any attention," Savannah said. "He just got embarrassed. Don't take what he said seriously."

But his hurtful words broke through a place in my heart that had already been cracked repeatedly over the years—a place that held how I viewed my body.

Nathan's cutting remark took me back to a litany of other

hurtful words. My mother had said, "Nona, you're as big as a house!" Elementary school classmates had called me "Miss Piggy." In middle school I was called "fatty pants" almost every day. I remembered feeling like the Michelin Man in Bongo shorts as I stared at myself in the dressing room mirror. When Nathan said I had a body that was only good for sex with the lights off, my heart wrapped itself around those words and held them tight.

Although Nathan said, "Nobody wants your *body*," my heart heard, "Nobody wants *you*." His toxic words melded with those other voices and reinforced a belief I had secretly held for many years: the belief that I wasn't wanted.

The Power of Words

The messages we send one another—whether verbally or through body language—have power. The wisdom writer said, "Death and life are in the power of the tongue" (Proverbs 18:21 KJV). The Hebrew word translated "power" is *yad*, which most commonly refers to the "forearm" or "hand." So this verse could also be read as, "Death and life are in the *hand* of the tongue."

Although every body part is needed, hands occupy an important role in creation. Hands fluff pillows and tuck us in at night, creating homes that provide us with comfort and warmth. Our hands give a hug or rub of the back, creating comfort during sadness and grief. Our hands create protection by locking doors to prevent intruders from entering our spaces. Our hands create security by tying our boats to a dock to prevent them from drifting away.

But the same hands that make us safe and secure are also

the ones that can wreak devastation. Hands pull triggers. Hands make bombs. Hands strangle necks. Hands punch in anger. And just as the hand of a body can create safety and security or create harm and insecurity, so does the hand of a tongue.

The word *insecure* means unprotected or not firmly secured. It is used in computer programming to describe a computer system that is exposed to attack because it is unprotected. It is used in finance to describe a loan that has a high risk of loss because it is not secured by a stable underlying asset. Fundamentally, that which is insecure is vulnerable.

Our understanding of who we are, our identity, is constantly being formed. From infancy to adulthood, the voices speaking over us shape our identity. My earliest memory of identity formation is having my kindergarten teacher, Mr. Russo, tell me, "Nona, you're so smart. You did a great job!" He smiled widely when he said it, and I wanted so badly to please him that I received his words in my heart with gladness. I worked to live up to his expectations, and I believed I was smart—until I changed schools for first grade.

After I did poorly on a spelling test, my first-grade teacher, Ms. Penny, said, "Nona, these words aren't hard. You must have a learning disability." She frowned deeply when she said it, so even though I didn't quite understand what a learning disability was, I figured it was the opposite of being smart. My heart received her words as truth, and I allowed them to displace what I previously believed from Mr. Russo. I began living down to meet her low expectations of me.

My teachers' words shaped my understanding of who I was because I had nothing else to go by. Even though I am a preacher and Bible teacher today, I didn't grow up in a Christian home.

I didn't have a parent affirming my worth by speaking God's Word over me, so I didn't know I could be anything other than what I was told. Sadly, the woman who should have used her words to create in me a secure view of my identity instead used her words to break me down.

My mother didn't want children. She told me numerous times that she didn't want *me*, specifically. She and my father had been married thirteen years when she found out she was pregnant, and she cried because she felt children were a burden. To make matters worse, although my father was elated to finally become a dad, he was diagnosed with terminal stomach cancer halfway through the pregnancy and passed away two months before my second birthday.

When I was four and five years old, my mother had a string of boyfriends who paraded through our lives until she met a guy who moved in with us. I didn't like him from the beginning, but she told me to give him a chance because he wasn't going anywhere. Not long after he moved in, he started sexually abusing me. After two years of repeated abuse, I finally worked up the courage to tell my mother. Although she had him locked up, she also took me with her on the day of his release from jail and brought him back home, where the abuse resumed.

The message I internalized when my mom allowed him back into our home was that I was both unwanted and unloved. If she loved me, how could my mother bring him back, knowing he had violated me? When the abuse resumed, I decided not to say anything because it was clear to me (and to him) that I didn't matter. Many years later, after I had graduated from college, I confronted my mother about it and asked her why she had let him abuse me. She said, "Well, it wouldn't have happened if you had kept your legs closed." In other words, it was my fault. I had been a five-year-old seductress. I had been an eight-year-old temptress. I had brought it on myself. Hearing my mother say those words hurt me because they reinforced the message that she didn't want me.

The craziest thing is that even though I was an adult when she said it, even though I had been in a relationship with Jesus for many years by then, and even though I knew it was a lie, it still made me question myself. *Did I do something to make him think I wanted it? Should I have fought back harder? Did I make him think it was okay?* My identity was still being formed by my mother's words, even after I had memorized Scripture about who God said I was in him. Even after I had preached multiple times about the importance of finding our identity in Christ. Even after I knew better. And this is how I know that what we *believe in our hearts* matters more than what we *know in our minds*. More on that in a moment.

When people say hurtful things to us, it damages our self-worth. And it can happen anywhere: for example, in the middle of a client meeting at work. Perhaps after working hard to pull together a stunning presentation, you discovered one miscalculation in the PowerPoint. In front of everyone, your manager said, "Sorry, everyone. This figure should be $267 million, not $267 thousand. I apologize for not checking this work before allowing it to be presented to you." As your manager rolled their eyes, you didn't shed a tear because your throat was so tight you could hardly breathe.

> What we *believe in our hearts* matters more than what we *know in our minds*.

Or maybe it was that time you were walking your dog and

your neighbor looked at you and said loudly, "I guess they're letting anyone rent here now." The tears flowed down your cheeks as you remembered how many times you had prayed as a child to grow up and move out of the projects, only to have people think you're not good enough to live in "their" neighborhood.

Maybe it was the time you were so excited to attend a special event that you bought a new dress in hopes of looking your best, only to have one of the attendees look you up and down and say, "Where in the world did you get that hideous thing?" with a look of disdain. You feigned a laugh, but when you returned home that night, you vowed never to dress to impress again.

These situations would be painful for even the most self-assured person. When people speak death over us instead of life, our identity takes a hit. It happened to my friend, Sarah.

Sarah has an incredible voice, one I heard by chance one day when she was trying to remember the name of a song and sang some of it so I could help her. She sounded like Celine Dion, and my jaw hit the floor. I had no idea something so beautiful could live within someone so quiet. Sarah is the stereotypical introvert. She never draws attention to herself and prefers doing anything that allows her to work alone.

"Sarah! Your voice is *amazing*!" I said. "Do you sing at church? You should!"

"Oh, no," she responded with a confused look on her face. "My voice is hideous. I wouldn't ever subject people to it," she laughed nervously.

"*Subject* people to it? Girl, you have a gift! Why don't you sing?" I asked.

"I used to sing but stopped in the fourth grade," she said.

"That was a long time ago. What happened?" I asked.

"Well, I was in my bedroom rehearsing for a solo for a school program, and I was really feeling the song, so I guess I was singing too loud," she said. "My mom came in and yelled at me and said I had a horrible voice and needed to shut up."

It had been years—10,950 days, to be exact—since her mother had told her she had a horrible voice, and Sarah *still* hadn't sung publicly. Although she added a laugh and was half joking, she told me she didn't even hum anymore because she didn't want to hurt people's ears with her voice. The fact that ten seconds of her mother's toxic words could create thirty years of silence in her shows the lethal power of the tongue. When words aren't handled with care, they can damage our identity.

While the sting of toxic words can catch us off guard and shock us, they can also cement a destructive belief we already hold about ourselves. While Nathan's words didn't surprise me, they shattered the place in my heart that had been repeatedly cracked through years of criticism about my body. Maybe you've experienced this as well.

When your husband said, "You've really packed on the pounds, haven't you?" it wasn't his observation alone that hurt. What hurt most was that his comment exposed the shame you already felt and had been trying to hide beneath the flowy dresses and blouses. When those words came tumbling off your husband's tongue, you felt like your secret shame was now on public display.

When your sister said, "You're *still* a cashier? Shouldn't you at least be a manager by now?" you weren't hurt only by her disapproval. What hurt most was that her comment exhumed the shame you already tried to bury deep beneath the smile you wore when people gushed about your sister, the doctor.

When your colleague said, "You haven't been invited to Dan's house yet?" it wasn't the exclusion alone that hurt. What hurt most was that their comment shone a spotlight on your history of being left out of social gatherings. Although you responded with, "It's fine," the pain you feel every time a group of colleagues shares an inside joke from their after-hours fun confirms that it's *not* fine.

The most painful thing about what your husband, sister, or colleague said is that it unearthed beliefs you already had about yourself. Hearing their words left you feeling exposed, vulnerable, and unprotected—insecure.

It has been twenty-five years since Nathan said those toxic words to me at that football game, but I can still hear the anger in his voice. I still remember the number 22 on the sleeve of his varsity baseball jacket. I still remember how the splash of freckles began floating in a sea of pink as embarrassment bloomed across his face. His words probably took up ten seconds in my day, but the insecurity they triggered in me would come to define the next ten years of my life.

The hurtful words of my mother and classmates cracked the foundation of my identity. Although their words were painful and left me in tears, Nathan's words landed on that already inse-cure foundation and demolished it. It wasn't until Nathan—the guy I had wanted to impress, the guy I had thought was cute and secretly hoped would like me—said those words that I took notice and felt the weight of accumulated shame. His swift and public rejection triggered me. It compelled me to look for evidence that I wasn't as bad as he said I was. But the more I looked around, the more I realized I didn't measure up.

I noticed that the cheerleaders were skinny *in comparison to me*, making me think, "How could I have ever thought I could become one of them? I'm as big as a house."

I also noticed that Savannah was gorgeous *in comparison to me*, making me think, "Did she become my friend because she felt sorry for me, the ugly, fat girl?"

Then I saw that Nathan was toned, handsome, and popular, making me think, "Of course he wouldn't like me! How could he like Miss Piggy?"

Although I was physically at the game, I was so distracted by my thoughts that I was mentally and emotionally in a different world. A world defined by my deficiencies. A world defined by my shortcomings. A world in which I felt wholly unprotected and vulnerable to a degree I had never felt before because a fear-filled question formed within me: *What if Nathan is right?*

The Mind-Heart Connection

I once attended a leadership seminar where the speaker said, "Thoughts lead to actions, actions lead to habits, habits lead to character, and character leads to destiny." It made a lot of sense at the time, but the more I've thought about this progression, the more I have come to believe a crucial step is missing between thoughts and actions. We have thoughts all day long, but we don't act on all of them.

If someone sent you a message that offered $5,000 if you sent them your social security number, you might initially think, "Wow, I could really use $5,000." But your thought alone wouldn't be enough to make you send the scammer your social security number. No, between thinking of how great it would be to get that $5,000 and typing your social security number into the keyboard, you would have to *believe* the offer was legitimate, that sending your social security number to them would result in receiving $5,000. Thoughts don't lead to actions unless you believe them to be true—and not only in your *rational* mind but also in your *feeling* heart.

We tend to think our beliefs live in the rational, cognitive parts of our brains, but the Bible points out a nuance that turns this belief on its head (no pun intended). It says, "For as he thinks in his heart, so is he" (Proverbs 23:7 NKJV). Wait. How can you think (have cognition) in your heart (the center of emotion)?

Author and educator Nathan Rutstein once observed, "Prejudice [is] an emotional commitment to ignorance."[2] I believe, however, that being emotionally committed to ignorance extends beyond issues of prejudice. For example, there are people living among us who believe the earth is flat. Even after the various scientific discoveries that point to the spherical nature of earth and even after satellite imagery shows the earth to be round, they believe the earth is flat and that "round earthers" are crazy. The facts, figures, and photographic evidence of a round earth don't change their mind because the mind is not where their belief resides. It resides in the heart.

"For as he thinks in his heart, so is he" means our beliefs are not simply a function of our cognition, they are also a function of our emotions. Our emotions can convince us to do things that our cognition doesn't even agree with. Like changing your ex-boyfriend's phone contact name to "Do Not Respond" after a breakup, only to respond the moment "Do Not Respond" sends a text with a heart emoji. Like taking a new job that requires travel you can't fulfill due to family obligations because you wanted that job before you had a family. Like using unhealthy methods to lose weight as quickly as possible because you believe you won't be beautiful until you wear a certain size.

Our minds are like an ocean filled with countless boats, and each boat carries thoughts based on others' messages about who we are. Although what we think ultimately determines what we believe, our emotions are the current that pushes thoughts toward our hearts. Once those thoughts enter our hearts and are accepted as truth, they become beliefs, and those beliefs shape our identity. Our beliefs about ourselves are reflections of the thoughts we have accepted as true. And the thoughts we accept as true are reflections of the voices we value.

The Core of Insecurity

Savannah and her dad drove me home after the game. I waved back at them as I opened my front door and they pulled away into the night. I walked quickly to my bedroom, closed the door, sat on my bed, and stared into the mirror leaning against the wall across from me. That morning, just sixteen hours earlier, I had smiled into that mirror as I smoothed out the new jean skirt I had been so proud to wear. Even though my stomach had bulged beneath the material and fat rolls spilled over my belt, I left for school feeling good about myself. Now the same mirror that had reflected my joy reflected something entirely different. There was nothing in that mirror worth smiling about. Tears flowed as I saw what Nathan saw. He was right. I knew in my head that I was more than just a body, but my heart told me that nobody could possibly want the person carrying this body around.

At the core of insecurity is the need to be worthy. When we feel worthy, we feel wanted and valued, but when a void of worthiness leaves us feeling unwanted, we become insecure. We allow others to tell us what to think about ourselves, and we see ourselves as worthy only to the extent that others agree or disagree.

Now when I look back at the incident with Nathan at the football game, I can see that his reaction was simply a manifestation of his own desire to be worthy in the eyes of his friends. Before he said those hurtful words, he noticed his friends were laughing at him. Now that I understand how important friends' approval is to a teenager, I can imagine that when Nathan's friends laughed at him, his confidence was shaken. He lashed out at me because his hurt stirred the insecurity in his own heart.

The saying "hurt people hurt people" is true because hurt people have insecure, vulnerable hearts. When an insecure heart feels that its fragile identity is threatened, it attacks the source of the threat. The night of the football game, the negative attention Nathan received from his friends was a threat to his identity. He probably wondered what it meant about him if a fat girl rejected his touch. He was handsome and athletic, the type of guy who had no problem getting a girl's attention. So if a girl who was overweight didn't want him, what did that make him? His belief that he was a ladies' man was challenged, so he attacked me and put me down to restore his momentarily shaken belief.

This insight has allowed me to look back on the football game incident and have compassion for Nathan, but it took me many years to get to that place. His words and the words of many others affected me deeply, which is how I've come to understand that what we believe in our minds doesn't matter as much as what we believe in our hearts.

Maybe you're like me and have heard sermon after sermon affirming your value in Christ, but the words sailed into your ear and floated aimlessly around the ocean of your mind, never making their way to your heart. When toxic beliefs are entrenched in our hearts, memorizing Scriptures about our awesomeness isn't enough to change them. This is why I want you to pause and take a moment to consider what you believe about yourself.

When you make a mistake, what do you think? When you're afraid, what do you tell yourself? When you feel abandoned, what do you believe? It is the talk track running through your mind and heart that exposes what you believe, so take a moment to reflect on what you believe before moving to the next chapter.

Recall

Just as the hand of a body can create safety and security or create harm and insecurity, so does the hand of a tongue.

What we *believe in our hearts* matters more than what we *know in our minds*.

That which is insecure is vulnerable.

Thoughts don't lead to actions unless you believe them to be true.

At the core of insecurity is the need to be worthy.

Receive

Blessed is the one
    who does not walk in step with the wicked

or stand in the way that sinners take
    or sit in the company of mockers,
but whose delight is in the law of the LORD,
    and who meditates on his law day and night.
That person is like a tree planted by streams of water,
    which yields its fruit in season
and whose leaf does not wither—
    whatever they do prospers. (Psalm 1:1–3)

Recite

Father, help me to identify the toxic thoughts I have allowed into my heart. Help me to discern the toxic lies that were spoken over me so many times that I started to believe they were true. Help me to see myself through your eyes and to know I lack nothing.

Reflect

As time and space allowed me to prayerfully reflect on what Nathan said, I grew to have compassion for him because I realized his reaction was rooted more in embarrassment than malice. As you consider the people who have spoken toxic, hurtful words over you, remember that "hurt people hurt people," and allow yourself to extend compassion to them if for no other reason than not wanting to become like them.

Chapter Three

YOU'RE NOT WORTHY
AS YOU ARE

This chapter recounts memories of a traumatic event that may trigger painful memories in those who have survived physical, sexual, or verbal abuse. If you feel anxious while reading, feel free to skip to chapter 4.

Y ou little whore!" My mother lunged at me with ferocity in her eyes. I was eight years old and had somehow managed to get in the middle of a fight she was having with her boyfriend. I didn't know what a whore was, but the way she said it told me it wasn't good. She choked me until something made her stop, and I managed to run to my room and lock the door. It was just a typical day in our dysfunctional household.

After bringing her boyfriend back home from prison, my mother became physically and verbally abusive to me. In fits of rage, she called me names while punching, slapping, or choking me. I didn't know how to process the abuse, so I began acting out in elementary school. It was the only way I knew how to release the pain. Instead of asking, "What happened to you, Nona?" teachers and school administrators punished me for my behavior. They called me a "problem child" and told me I had a learning disability. I was told something was wrong with me so often by so many people that I believed them. I allowed their voices to shape my understanding of who I was.

Though we don't have a sense of our identity when we're born, the words spoken to us in our formative years tremendously influence how we come to define ourselves. And it happens in any number of ways.

After searching everywhere in your room, you asked your dad if he'd seen your favorite stuffed animal, only to have him sigh and snap, "You're always losing things! You're so forgetful." You were six. But even at forty-three you explain misplacing your keys by saying, "I'm forgetful. Always have been."

After discovering food particles on a plate you washed, your mom shoved it in your face and said, "How did you miss this on the plate? You're so lazy!" You were ten. But even at thirty-seven you have a list of dreams you've never pursued because you tell yourself, "That will take more energy than a slacker like me can give."

After bombing your geometry test for the second time, your teacher asked you to stay after class and said, "Math is not your strong suit." You were fifteen. But even as a twenty-year-old college student who wants to be an engineer, you've chosen education as your major because you think, "I'm not good at math."

THE LIES THEY TOLD ME

The words significant adults use to describe you in childhood and adolescence eventually become the words you use to describe yourself as an adult. The very tone of their voices can make our hearts race or calm down. We assign so much weight to their voices that the power of their words can make us feel protected or vulnerable, secure or insecure.

The words several of my teachers used made me believe I didn't only *have* a problem, I *was* a problem. There wasn't something wrong *with* me; *I* was wrong. After accepting their words as truth, I lived down to their expectations, creating a cycle of bad behavior that only reinforced their low opinion of me. The worse I behaved, the more critical the voices became until I hit bottom and couldn't fall any lower.

At nine years old, I decided to end my life. I wasn't sure what was on the other side of death, but the pain and worthlessness I felt were overwhelming. I had watched a talk show that told the story of a toddler who had died after drinking bleach. We didn't have any bleach, so I drank laundry detergent and assumed it would produce the same outcome. Instead, I ended up vomiting, but that was the extent of it. At age eleven, I took a knife to my left wrist and sliced it open, but I missed the artery, so the wound bled some but eventually clotted and stopped bleeding. I cleaned up the sink I had been leaning over, wrapped my wrist with a washcloth, lay down on my bed, and drifted off to sleep with a dull headache.

Although my suicide attempts were (fortunately) unsuccessful, the toxic words of my mother, her boyfriend, and others killed any sense of value I had, communicating that I was something to discard, something to use, something unworthy of love.

My mother often reminded me that I was a burden. She said

things like, "You're selfish! All you do is take, take, take! I wish I never had you." I carried that guilt into adulthood. I wouldn't ask people for help even when I really needed it because I didn't want to be a burden.

Several teachers blamed my acting out on a character deficiency. One day my fifth-grade teacher pulled me out of line on the way to art class and said, "You're never going to be anything! You make trouble for everybody." I had been acting out in her class that day—making jokes, talking back, and trying to be funny. I didn't know that trauma often works its way out of us through various means of expression and that what I needed was therapy and safety. I simply wore the "problem child" label I was given as if it were a coat. No one ever asked me why I behaved the way I did, so I simply accepted the indictment that I was broken and carried it with me into adulthood.

I recently came across a Kaiser Permanente study exploring the link between negative childhood experiences and well-being later in life. The study found a strong causal link between childhood trauma and the risk of delinquency, substance abuse, and poor health outcomes in adulthood. Because of their findings, researchers created an adverse childhood experiences assessment that ranks the probability of poor outcomes in adulthood based on childhood trauma. The assessment scale ranges from zero to ten, with ten indicating the highest probability of poor outcomes. When I took the assessment, I scored an eight.

True or false, toxic words reverberate in our hearts long after they are spoken.

Hurtful Words Add Up

As I stared at my reflection in the mirror the night Nathan told me I had a body nobody wanted, his words played on a loop in my mind: "What are you screaming for? I don't want you! With a body like that, you're not good for anything but sex with the lights off, anyway."

With every loop, I cried harder. I had been delusional to think I looked cute that morning, and every other morning before it. I thought about how no boy had ever sent me a note telling me he liked me or asked me to be his girlfriend or asked me to go on a date.

"I'm fat and ugly and no one wants me," I told myself as I stared into the mirror, tears blurring my vision.

As far back as I can remember, my classmates had made me the butt of their weight jokes. "Oink, oink, oink," my fourth-grade classmate Blake said through a wide smile. "Nona is Miss Piggy! Fatty pants! Fatty pants!" "It's getting too tight in here," my eighth-grade classmate Renatta said while looking straight at me when I walked into class late one day. "I can't breathe around all of this fat in my face!" I accepted their view of me as "fat" for years, even when I no longer was.

Nathan's words made me feel like something had literally broken inside me. The words my mother and others had spoken over me had cracked my heart, but Nathan's words were the blow that broke it. The effect of hurtful words is cumulative. And they accumulate in adulthood just as easily as they do in childhood.

Although you are exhausted at the end of a jam-packed day, you spend several hours preparing a dish for the office potluck the next day. A snarky colleague takes one bite of your dish and says with a laugh, "Yuck! Who brought in the dog food?" Although the comment was meant as a joke, you excuse yourself to the restroom to cry. You decide to overlook the colleague's rudeness and chalk up the comments to having different food preferences.

A couple of weeks later, you invite your mother over for dinner only to have her look at the food you lovingly prepared and say, "Lord, you call this a meal? I'm ordering takeout." Your daughter then says, "Call me when it's here," and bounds up the stairs to her room. The words of your mother and daughter are crushing, and you hide the pain behind a forced laugh. But you try to let it go and convince yourself that your mom was just trying to help.

The following week you make a cake for your best friend's birthday and even wrap it in a pretty box. Unfortunately, the box falls over during the drive to her house. When she opens the box, she says, "Aw, thank you. It's so . . . interesting." You burst into tears and yell, "I did my best! I'm so tired of my best not being good enough!" Since she doesn't have the context of the prior hurtful experiences, she opens her eyes wide and says, "Girl, stop being so sensitive. You always take things so personally. It's not a big deal." Maybe it's not a big deal by itself, but when hurtful incidents add up, the sum of those experiences *is* a big deal.

Hurtful words often leave cracks before they cause shatters. The compounding effect of hurtful words from your colleague, mother, daughter, and best friend creates a concentration of pain that acquires the strength of an emotional hurricane. When that hurricane batters your already-cracked heart, it shatters, surprising your best friend, and probably you too. The pain of hurtful words builds and builds until your heart breaks. That is what happened to me.

As I sat on the bed staring at myself, I suddenly felt an overwhelming urge to act. I *had* to lose weight, and fast. But I didn't know the first thing about weight loss. A few days later, while watching Geraldo Rivera's talk show, I came across the perfect solution. Or so I thought. The episode focused on eating disorders, and each of Geraldo's guests shared their personal struggles and the motivations behind them. Women who were nothing but skin and bones talked about something called anorexia. They didn't eat food because they were deathly afraid of gaining weight.

> Hurtful words often leave cracks before they cause shatters.

"Aha!" I thought. "That's it. I'll just stop eating. Problem solved."

Unfortunately, my body didn't agree with my mind's decision. A few hours into my starvation strategy, my stomach was rumbling like crazy. My resolve went down with the sun that day, and I ate a hearty dinner of two heaping plates of spaghetti, washed it down with multiple glasses of cranberry juice, and ate half a pack of cookies for dessert. As always.

I woke up the next day feeling like a failure. How was I going to lose weight if I couldn't stop eating for even one day? How could I drop the pounds I desperately needed to if I couldn't stop eating enough food to feed a family of four in one sitting?

I walked to the bathroom to shower, and after turning on the water to let it heat up, I glanced at the toilet and remembered an image I had seen on Geraldo's show: a woman kneeling in front of a toilet. The woman had shared her struggle with bulimia, a condition that caused her to gorge on food and then throw up to avoid getting fat. I had vomited a few times before, but it was always involuntary and the result of illness. I had never forced myself to throw up, but she had explained how she did it. I wondered, "Could this work for me?"

I grabbed a towel from under the sink, rolled it up in front of the toilet, and knelt before the porcelain commode as if it were an altar. I gagged myself until I threw up and repeated the process five times. It was horrible. My throat burned from the acid, and my eyes stung from the droplets that forced themselves out of my tear ducts. I felt the urge to cough several times but stifled it out of fear my mother might walk in and find me kneeling in front of the toilet with red eyes and food particles on the sides of my mouth.

When I finished, I flushed the toilet, stood up, rinsed my mouth, and brushed my teeth. My stomach felt empty, and my heart felt light. I looked into the mirror and smiled for the first time since Nathan's words at the football game.

"I can be as skinny as those cheerleaders if I keep this up," I thought. "I could be as pretty as Savannah if I keep this up. I could end up with a boyfriend like Nathan if I keep this up."

A sense of control washed over me because my decision would get me closer to the ideal I compared myself to. And it was intoxicating. But hindsight has helped me understand that instead of being *in* control, I had instead *relinquished* control to the power of toxic comparison. I had secured my identity to winning people's approval of my physical appearance, leading me to believe the lie that I wasn't worthy unless and until I measured up to their ideal. I believed the lie that I wasn't worthy until I was like someone else. Although I thought I was in control, I wasn't. The lie of toxic comparison was calling the shots.

The Two Types of Comparison

My struggles with food and weight continued well into adulthood. When I finally decided to begin a healthy weight-loss journey almost a decade ago, I weighed nearly three hundred pounds. One day I stumbled across a YouTube video series of a woman my age who had lost one hundred pounds and kept it off for years. The way she described feeling defeated at the beginning of her journey resonated with me at the cellular level, so I spent hours watching every video she had. With every new video, I felt what I can only describe as a breath of fresh air for my spirit. It made me believe that if she could do it, so could I.

Comparison can take two forms in our lives—inspiration and expiration. When we breathe oxygen into our lungs, it's a *physiological* process called inspiration. When another person's success moves our intellect or emotions, it's a *psychological* process called inspiration. Healthy comparison inspires. One of the reasons I love the "We're debt free!" scream on Dave Ramsey's nationally syndicated radio show is because the stories of people paying off their debts inspire others to make better financial choices. Hearing success stories gives hope to listeners who feel they are in more debt than they could ever pay off. Healthy comparison invites them to believe they can be successful too.

When my husband and I listened to the people on Ramsey's

show who had paid off hundreds of thousands of dollars in debt, we said to each other, "We don't have as much debt as they do, so we should be able to do that too!" And we did. Healthy comparison leads to inspiration. And when we face challenges, we all need inspiration to stay the course in pursuit of our goals and dreams.

But then there is the unhealthy, or toxic, form of comparison. While breathing oxygen into our lungs is inspiration, exhaling it is expiration. And do you know what else *expiration* means? It means to die. While healthy comparison invigorates us and breathes life into the vision we have for ourselves and our families, toxic comparison debilitates us and sucks life out of that vision. It does this by causing us to see another person's success as our failure.

> Healthy comparison leads to inspiration.

Healthy comparison inspires us and produces motivation and joy, but toxic comparison "expires" us and produces exhaustion and anxiety. Toxic comparison seeps into our hearts like a poison and kills our sense of worthiness. It feeds us the lie that we need to be like someone else to matter. Instead of inspiring us to become better, toxic comparison convinces us we aren't worthy. Toxic comparison is death-dealing.

When you feel like your marriage is failing and friends at church constantly talk about how beautiful Mary's family is, toxic comparison leads you to curate a fictional image of your perfect family on Instagram. Instead of inspiring you to seek counseling with your husband to fix what's broken in your marriage, toxic comparison compels you to expend your energy on trying to make your life look like it's perfect. But since you know the truth, the momentary pleasure you get every time someone likes one of your posts quickly expires in the harsh reality that your husband has walked by you all day without speaking. Again.

When you feel like others get more attention than you, toxic comparison leads you to lease your lifestyle on credit to fabricate an "I have it all in Jesus's name" image. You caption a photo of you wearing Christian Louboutin heels with, "Yea, though I walk through the valley of the shadow of death, I will fear no evil," though the main point of your post is that you're walking through that valley in red-bottom heels. You desperately want the likes and comments that make you feel worthy, but your temporary feeling of "I made it" is snuffed out every time you think about your massive Mastercard debt.

Toxic comparison causes us to secure our confidence to things in which we are least confident. When you feel like you haven't achieved enough in your own right, toxic comparison compels you to to create a fictional image of being well liked and powerful. You never let a celebrity photo op go to waste and are always ready to snap a quick "usie" that screams, "Hey! See who I'm with? I matter!" But the reality of not actually knowing that person makes every "That's so cool!" comment feel hollow. Your sense of achievement expires in light of what you haven't actually achieved.

Poisonous Words

For much of my life, what I felt least confident about was my body. I struggled with bulimia for a decade after Nathan's comment triggered my downward spiral. I lost weight because of my eating disorder and gained the attention of boys in high school as I slimmed down. But when I looked in the mirror, the reflection staring back at me never changed. I went from a size sixteen to a size ten, but at my lowest weight, I still saw the girl who had stared back at me through tear-filled eyes the night of the football game. This mental health condition is called body dysmorphic disorder and to this day, I am one of the millions of people who struggle with it.

Even as I slimmed down in high school and heard people say things like, "Looking good, Nona!" their compliments felt good only in the moment. When I saw myself in the mirror, I didn't see anything good. I saw only my flaws—the belly fat that spilled ever so slightly over the top of my jeans, the stretch marks on my arms that peeked out from my short-sleeve shirts, and the chest I apparently inherited from my father because it was flat as a board. Unlike a Snapchat filter that makes everything look better, toxic comparison is a deficiency filter that makes everything look worse. It causes us to see only what we lack, even when we have so much. I believed I was deficient, and as long as I believed that, nothing could change my mind. The reason nothing could change my mind was because my mind wasn't where my belief lived. My belief lived in my heart.

> Toxic comparison is a deficiency filter that makes everything look worse.

The voices that poisoned my view of my body made me believe I would be worthy only if I were skinny. I didn't have the assurance that I had value regardless of my weight. I knew only that the people who mattered most to me felt I wasn't good enough as I was.

When I got married, I felt confident in the love my husband had for me. As a result, I didn't feel the need to continue the unhealthy practices that caused me to slim down. But within a few years, I had gained back all the weight I'd lost—with interest. Ultimately, I tipped the scales at 276 pounds and wore a size twenty. Although my husband never said anything about my weight and loved me the same as he did when we first got married, I didn't feel good emotionally, mentally, or physically.

Walking was difficult, my joints ached, and I didn't like how my clothes fit. I wanted a change, so I decided to educate myself on weight loss and do it the healthy way. After being inspired by the weight loss videos I had started watching on YouTube, one weekend in early 2013, I bought and read *Weight Loss for Dummies* (really). Then I cleaned out my pantry and stocked my refrigerator with healthy food options. I bought a gym membership and signed up to run a half-marathon. I wasn't a runner (not even a walker), but I did it because I wasn't playing any games!

Within six months of eating healthy and working out consistently, I dropped sixty pounds. It was the hardest thing I'd ever done, but I was on a high from my results, so I stuck with my regimen. Six months later, I had dropped another forty pounds for a total of one hundred pounds lost! I felt amazing. I went from wearing a size twenty to wearing a size eight, and I've maintained my weight loss for more than eight years. But even now when I look in the mirror, I don't naturally see a size-eight woman looking back at me. Instead, I see every fat roll, stretch mark, and imperfection. I have to strip away the false layers of visual memories to excavate the woman I am today.

A toxin is a substance that, when introduced to a living organism, disrupts its metabolic processes. It can do so quickly or slowly, but the result is always a form of death. For example, victims of a coral snake bite experience slurred speech and blurred vision, and the tissue surrounding the bite experiences necrosis, death of the living cells. If the venom is left untreated, the victim can end up paralyzed, blind, or dead.

Just as toxic substances can kill people, toxic words can kill people too. Poisonous words damage our identity. If I don't apply an antivenom of truth to what I see in the mirror every day, I still see an overweight body I no longer have.

For many years, wanting to be wanted shaped my sense of worthiness, but even after marriage provided evidence of being wanted, I had not yet healed the core wound within me that produced my insecurity. It would take another experience to bring me face-to-face with what lived in my heart and to set me on the path to healing and freedom for good.

Recall

Toxic words reverberate in our hearts long after they are spoken.

The effect of hurtful words is cumulative.

Healthy comparison leads to inspiration.

Hurtful words often leave cracks before they cause shatters.

Instead of inspiring us to become better, toxic comparison convinces us we aren't worthy.

Toxic comparison causes us to secure our confidence to things in which we are least confident.

Toxic comparison is a deficiency filter that makes everything look worse.

Poisonous words damage our identity.

Receive

Do not conform to the pattern of this world, but be transformed by the renewing of your mind. Then you will be able to test and approve what God's will is—his good, pleasing and perfect will. (Romans 12:2)

Recite

Father, help me identify any toxic comparison in my life. Help me see the toxic behaviors, beliefs, and attitudes I have allowed to define me. Unmask the lies that tell me I am not worthy unless I become more like someone else. Help me to know that you made me worthy.

Reflect

The person we often have the most difficulty forgiving is ourselves. As you become aware of the ways toxic comparison has manifested itself in your behaviors, extend the same compassion to yourself that you would extend to a friend. Remind yourself that you did what you thought was right at the time, and commit to charting a new course.

Part Two

THE SOURCES OF OUR INSECURITY

Chapter Four

WHO DO YOU SAY I AM?

"O h my goodness! Did you see Laura's new boyfriend? They look so happy and cute together!" My friend's text confused me. Laura lived in Atlanta, Georgia. I lived in Gainesville, Florida. Of course I hadn't seen her new boyfriend.

"No, I haven't. Are you in Atlanta? Tell her I said hi, and let her know I miss her."

"I'm not in Atlanta, girl," my friend responded. "I'm talking about her Facebook post. Have you seen it?"

"Oh! No. I'm not on Facebook."

"What! Nona, girl, how are you *not* on Facebook? You're missing out!"

Facebook launched the year I graduated from college. I heard occasional rumblings about it but didn't feel compelled to join until a few years later. As I reflect on the period before I signed up for an account, I clearly remember that if I wasn't hanging out with someone, I had no idea what they were doing, when they were doing it, where they were doing it, or with whom they were doing it. And I didn't care either.

I didn't know who was wearing which designer to an exclusive event I had never heard of, nor was I aware of which couples were enjoying the breathtaking views of Santorini or toasting the sunset with champagne flutes at the exclusive St. Regis Bora Bora Resort (#couplegoals). And I don't remember wondering about any of that either because out of sight, out of mind.

The only people whose whereabouts mattered to me were those with whom I needed to meet face-to-face or speak with for a specific purpose. I had no reason to peer into the lives of anyone other than the group of people whose presence, actions, and decisions affected my day-to-day life.

While in college, I had joined an early social network called BlackPlanet, but it consisted only of chat rooms where people discussed countless topics in a live stream of text. I had a profile page where I added a picture and minimal information about myself, but it was truly information only—there were no status updates. BlackPlanet was simply a forum for conversations.

I joined Myspace when it became a thing, but after creating my profile, I never went back and checked it. I was busy living my life as a microbiology major at the University of Florida, with a heavy course load of chemistry, calculus, biology, and practical labs. I was active in several on-campus organizations and clubs, and when I wanted to catch up with friends, we simply met in person on Turlington Plaza or called each other on our cell phones (back when people used their cell phones to actually call people).

I remember being part of various listservs, which were essentially the email versions of WhatsApp or GroupMe threads. By the time I created a Facebook account, I was married and already an executive, so I didn't post much and was focused on living life offline. I only joined because friends constantly referred to Facebook posts when mentioning how cute so-and-so's baby was or how happy so-and-so looked in their new job at XYZ corporation.

I recently reviewed my archived posts from my early days using Facebook. They were either photos of my food (#foodie) or a few sentences opining about the events of the day. For example, when my oldest son was only a few months old, I made a 2:00 a.m. post that said, "Nona Jones is up past her bedtime because her baby boy apparently doesn't believe in such things." I didn't share pictures of myself and don't recall other people sharing many either.

At that point, I had a digital camera I had to connect to a computer to upload any photos I took. Even when camera phones came out, taking a selfie wasn't easy. At the time, phones had only a rear-facing camera. If you wanted a picture of yourself, you had two options: (1) turn your phone backward and try to guess where the button was to snap the photo while simultaneously smiling and positioning yourself in an unseen frame or (2) ask someone else to take the picture, which felt super vain if you weren't with someone else. For the second option, you could avoid the discomfort by either inviting someone to be in the picture with you (#usie) or by grabbing a random object (a book, plant, coffee cup, anything to deflect the vanity) and pretending you wanted a picture with it. But when the front-facing camera came along, everything changed.

Front-facing cameras allowed you to shed any pretense for why you wanted to take a picture of yourself. You took a picture *of* yourself *by* yourself *for* yourself. It was the outgrowth of a phenomenon known as "feeling yourself." For my colloquially challenged friends, "feeling yourself" means you feel good because you look good. Your hair was looking good, your makeup was looking good, and your outfit was looking good, so you decided to memorialize the moment. But leaving that photo in your phone's camera roll wasn't enough when there were other people who could see how good you looked too. Enter the #selfie post.

My first selfie post was an image of me sitting in my office. I had been working on a report that was draining my intellectual reserves, so I pulled out my phone and typed a status update that said, "Brain on E," *E* for *exhaustion*. Then I had the idea to include a photo of myself to illustrate my sentiment. I held up my phone, switched the camera to face front, sighed deeply, and snapped the picture. I didn't take multiple pictures. I didn't even *think* to take multiple pictures. I took just one picture and added it to my post. The next day, I went to Facebook to post about my lunch when I noticed a dozen people had liked my selfie post and had commented, "So beautiful," "You look so good in that color," "Love your hair," and more.

I was shocked. It never occurred to me that people would comment on my appearance based on a post about my intellectual exhaustion. In fact, it never occurred to me that people would comment at all. But something stirred in me when I read those comments. Each compliment felt like a warm, cuddly blanket. I read and reread those comments because they felt good. And after every reading, I felt an invisible thread pulling my attention back to that post to see if there were more comments and likes. I was pleasantly surprised to find that there usually were.

As I climbed into bed that night and rested my head on the pillow, I had a smile on my face. I also had a thought in my heart as I closed my eyes: "What should I post tomorrow to get more likes?" But deep down, the real question rolling around in my soul was slightly different: "What should I post tomorrow to get people to like *me*?"

Insecurity leads us to equate attention with worth.

In a fascinating recent study of "selfitis" (the clinical term for an addiction to selfies), researchers interviewed a group of four hundred students and learned that more than half (223 respondents) reported taking between one and four selfies a day, with more than a quarter (141) taking between five and eight selfies per day. When asked why, students said things like, "I gain enormous attention by sharing my selfies on social media," and, "Taking different selfie poses helps increase my social status."[3]

> Insecurity leads us to equate attention with worth.

Insecurity causes our hearts to tally the number of likes on our social media posts as a representation of our worth.

The first time people responded positively to my appearance on social media, it was a pleasant surprise that left me feeling a bit better about myself. Reading those comments changed the way I saw myself that day. And therein lies the insidious power of comparison. Comparison changes the way you see yourself because it can cause you to see yourself through the eyes of others. Their view eclipses what you see with your own eyes. For example, while I saw myself as exhausted, others saw me as beautiful. However, when others disapprove of what they see, those negative views can also eclipse what you see. While you might see a woman aging gracefully or a college student learning from mistakes or a mother doing her best or a guy putting forth the effort to find a job after getting fired, others might see wrinkles, failure, disappointment, and broken promises. When we see ourselves through the eyes of others, we make others the source of our worthiness.

To illustrate this point, I want to explore a Bible story that may be familiar to you. It's the story of Israel's first two kings, Saul and David. We'll follow their story through the next several chapters, so I want to share some background details that may seem a bit weighty, but trust me, they're necessary.

Saul and David

Saul was the son of a man named Kish. Various Bible translations describe Saul's dad as a man of "standing," "power," "stalwart character," and "influence and wealth" (1 Samuel 9:1). One day Kish's donkeys wandered off, so he tasked Saul with going to look for them: "Take one of the servants with you and go and look for the donkeys" (1 Samuel 9:3). Now, the fact that his dad said to take *one* of the servants meant there were *many* servants, and having donkeys (plural) indicates that Kish was a wealthy man. Therefore, so was Saul.

Saul set out with one of the servants to search for the missing donkeys. Unbeknownst to him, God had told a prophet named Samuel that Saul was coming to see him and that Saul was to be anointed king of Israel. When Saul showed up, Samuel invited him to stay and eat with him and then added, "As for the donkeys you lost three days ago, do not worry about them; they have been found. And to whom is all the desire of Israel turned, if not to you and your whole family line?" (1 Samuel 9:20).

Saul was flabbergasted. Stunned. I can imagine him thinking, "Huh? I just came here looking for our donkeys. Why would a prophet ask me to stay for a couple of days if the donkeys have been found? Wait a minute. What did he say about my family? That all the desire of Israel has turned toward us? What? What is he saying?" After gathering his thoughts, Saul said, "But am I not a Benjamite, from the smallest tribe of Israel, and is not my clan the least of all the clans of the tribe of Benjamin? Why do you say such a thing to me?" (1 Samuel 9:21).

> Sometimes toxic comparison diminishes us by making us small in our own eyes.

There were twelve tribes of Israel, and each tribe was named for one of the sons of a patriarch named Jacob, whose name was later changed to Israel. Before his death, Israel (Jacob) had blessed each of his twelve sons. Since Benjamin was the youngest son, he was blessed last. Although his tribe ended up being the smallest, the Benjamites were mighty and well resourced. Unfortunately, despite the resources Saul's tribe had, comparing himself to the other tribes caused him to see himself as lacking. Sometimes toxic comparison diminishes us by making us small in our own eyes.

I have read Saul's response to Samuel countless times. It is this very response that inspired me to write this book because it puzzled me. Consider these facts from Saul's story:

- Saul told Samuel he didn't understand why all of Israel's desire was turned toward him and his family.
- Saul believed his family occupied an insignificant position among the tribes of the nation of Israel.
- Saul's story begins by stating that Saul's family was

one of "standing," "power," "stalwart character," and "influence and wealth."

This begs the question of where Saul got the idea that he came from an inconsequential and unimportant family. Why did he think he was less-than, not good enough, and didn't measure up? Wherever the idea came from, his unwillingness to let go of it would cost him the kingdom just a few decades later.

Saul's eventual downfall as king was rooted in insecurity-fueled disobedience. God had instructed Saul to obliterate a population of people known as the Amalekites (1 Samuel 15). Many generations earlier, the Amalekites had attacked Israel when they were tired, weak, and vulnerable during their wilderness journey out of Egypt (Exodus 17:8–16). Saul was not only to kill the Amalekites but also to destroy everything they owned. But instead of obeying God, Saul caved when his soldiers pressured him to keep rather than destroy the good stuff—the best cattle, the best sheep, and more.

Big mistake.

The Lord sent the prophet Samuel to pronounce judgment: "Because you have rejected the word of the LORD, he has rejected you as king" (1 Samuel 15:23). Saul's heart dropped, and he tried to rationalize his decision: "I was afraid of the men and so I gave in to them" (1 Samuel 15:24). After decades of occupying the role and identity of king of Israel, Saul still saw himself as the kid who came from the most insignificant clan in the smallest tribe of Israel. He had more money, power, influence, and standing than anyone else in Israel, but it wasn't enough. He couldn't see past who he had *been* despite who he had *become*. Toxic comparison filters our present identity through our past deficiencies.

"Although you were once small in your own eyes," Samuel responded, "did you not become the head of the tribes of Israel? The LORD anointed you king over Israel" (1 Samuel 15:17). The kingdom was ultimately taken from Saul because, even after all God had done to change Saul's identity, he had secured his identity to the fickle affirmation of other human beings. He wanted their applause more than he wanted God's approval. And because of this, God told Samuel it was time to anoint a new king.

The story goes on to introduce a new family, the family of Jesse of Bethlehem. In contrast to the way Kish, Saul's father, was introduced, the text uses no flowery words to describe Jesse. He is simply introduced as "Jesse of Bethlehem" (1 Samuel 16:1).

At God's command, Samuel traveled to Bethlehem and asked to meet Jesse's sons. Samuel knew God had chosen one of Jesse's sons to be king, but he didn't know which one. After Jesse introduced seven of his sons, God told Samuel that none of them were to be anointed king. So Samuel asked Jesse if there were any additional sons. "Yeah, the youngest is out there tending sheep," Jesse responded. Jesse sent for him, and when young David stood before Samuel, God affirmed, "This is the one" (1 Samuel 16:12).

Although we might expect David to be perplexed and have questions, Scripture records no response from him to these surprising events. Under the same circumstances that led Saul to question his worthiness, David appears to suffer no self-doubt. Just as every word of Scripture is intentional, I also believe every *missing* word is intentional. I will not add to what is missing, but I invite you to take an imaginary journey with me for a moment.

Imagine your teenage self, minding your business and mowing your parents' grass when one of your siblings comes outside and says, "Hey, Dad wants you." You stop, turn off the lawn mower, and make your way inside the house. Standing there are your seven siblings and your father. All eyes are on you when an unknown, gray-haired man walks toward you. When he reaches you, he says nothing, pulls out a bottle of olive oil, and pours it over your head. When the last drop slides down your forehead, he turns to the group and pronounces, "Introducing the new king of Israel."

What might you think? Perhaps something like, "Huh?" Or, "Why me?" Or maybe, "This is interesting."

What's significant is how David's thinking differs from Saul's thinking. Specifically, how David *doesn't* ask Samuel the question Saul had asked, which was a question rooted in the *opinion* of others. A question rooted in the *valuation* of others. A question rooted in *comparison* to others. In contrast to Saul, David does not ask, "Why would you anoint me king?" Instead, the Bible simply says, "From that day on the Spirit of the LORD came powerfully upon David" (1 Samuel 16:13–14). Meanwhile, the Spirit had departed from Saul.

> Your identity is secure when you believe that what God says about you is true.

God had chosen both men to be king, but while Saul secured his identity to who others said he was, David secured his identity to who God said he was. Your identity is secure when you believe that what God says about you is true.

Nothing to Be Insecure About

While I've never been surprise-anointed for royal leadership, I have had something so unbelievable happen to me that it left me speechless. I was sitting in a church in Birmingham, Alabama, waiting to meet with the pastor when my cell phone rang. Caller ID indicated it was a number from Dallas, Texas, that I didn't recognize, but I answered since I had some time on my hands.

"Hi, Mrs. Jones?" a woman's voice inquired.

"Hi, yes," I said.

"I have Bishop T. D. Jakes on the line for you," she said.

My eyebrows furrowed in confusion, wondering whether this was a prank.

Then Bishop Jakes's unmistakable voice broke the silence. "Hi, Nona. Thanks for taking my call."

I was stunned.

"Um, hi. Yes, of course," I stammered.

"Listen," he said, "I'm calling because I'm putting together a roster of influential women to speak at my upcoming Woman, Thou Art Loosed master class, and your name was given to me as highly recommended. Would you consider joining me?"

Although I am fluent in English, I couldn't understand what he was saying. My mind flooded with questions: "Me? How did he get my number? Is this real? Me!"

Fortunately, the response that came out was more coherent. "Yes, sir. I would be honored."

As much as I couldn't believe what had just happened, I also didn't scour the web to see who else had been invited to speak. I didn't think to ask him who else had been considered. I simply accepted the invitation and was honored to be included. At that point in my life, I think I had fewer than one thousand Instagram followers. I had not published any books. I had not yet been exposed to others' success enough to even compare myself to them. So, like young David, all I thought to do was to be grateful and receive the opportunity as the gift it was.

In the absence of comparison, we have nothing to be insecure about.

Which Voice Will You Believe?

We'll come back to the story of Saul and David, but first I want to explore another fascinating story about identity in the Bible, this one from the life of Jesus.

Jesus once asked his disciples, "Who do people say the Son of Man is?" The disciples responded, "Some say John the Baptist; others say Elijah; and still others, Jeremiah or one of the prophets" (Matthew 16:13–14). Jesus then asked one of the simplest yet most profound questions in Scripture: "But what about you? Who do *you* say I am?" (Matthew 16:15, emphasis added).

The twelve disciples had spent almost every waking moment with Jesus for a couple of years at that point. They had witnessed him heal people, perform countless miracles, and teach with authority in the presence of the Pharisees and Sadducees. If anyone should've known who Jesus was, it should have been them, right? They saw his power with their *own eyes*, heard his words with their *own ears*. And yet when Peter rightly responded, "You are the Messiah, the Son of the living God," Jesus replied, "Blessed are you, Simon son of Jonah, for *this was not revealed to you by flesh and blood*, but by my Father in heaven" (Matthew 16:16–17, emphasis added).

Here is why Jesus's statement is so profound: The people who saw and heard Jesus identified him as John the Baptist, Elijah, or Jeremiah because they compared Jesus's ministry and teaching to that of these men. They identified Jesus based on who he reminded them of. We do something similar when we identify people based on who they remind us of. We say our daughter is cheerful like Aunt Sally, or our boss is mean and gruff like our old volleyball coach. We tend to identify people based on our sensory experience—what we see, hear, touch, or smell—and how it reminds us of someone else. This is part of what makes Jesus's question profound. He wanted to share this truth: *people's experience of you is not who you are.* Just as Jesus wasn't John the Baptist, Elijah, Jeremiah, or one of the prophets, you aren't who other people say you are. Jesus essentially said, "I am more than what you see me do. I am more than what you hear me say. I am more than what you feel when I'm around. *I am who the Father says I am—and so are you.*"

Many people think comparison causes insecurity, which is why many self-help and self-esteem books try to use positive affirmations to help you stop comparing yourself with others. But affirmations don't work long term because they don't address the root of the problem. Comparison does not *cause* insecurity; comparison *results* from insecurity. Insecurity causes comparison because when our identity is secured to the unstable, ever-changing opinions of others, we think the only way to increase our value is to become whatever they think we should be.

Your mother says, "Your sister always does so well in math. Why are you struggling?" You respond by setting your sister's performance in math as the benchmark for academic success.

Your friend says, "Maybe more squats will make your legs

more toned like Barbara's." You respond by setting Barbara's muscular legs as the benchmark for fitness success.

Your husband says, "Your mother takes such great care of your father. She irons his clothes and always has a hot meal ready." You respond by setting your mother as the benchmark for being a good wife.

Your manager says, "You're coming across as combative when you disagree with people. James has a more conciliatory approach when he disagrees with colleagues." You respond by setting James as the benchmark for professional success.

You begin to secure aspects of your identity to the good things people say about others and then measure how far you are from their standard. To please your mother, friend, husband, and manager, you give their voices credibility in your heart. You believe what they say and compare yourself to the ideal person in hopes of being more like them.

God, on the other hand, says this:

> [You are] fearfully and wonderfully made.
> (Psalm 139:14)

> Before I formed you in the womb I knew you,
> before you were born I set you apart.
> (Jeremiah 1:5)

> People look at the outward appearance, but the LORD looks at the heart. (1 Samuel 16:7).

God says all this without the qualifier of comparison. Which raises the question, Which voice will we believe? The voices of other human beings or the voice of God? Insecurity emerges when we believe the voices that diminish our value in comparison to others.

When God spoke a new identity over Saul, instead of believing God, Saul chose to believe the voices that had told him he was less than others. He essentially said to God, "Do you not know how insignificant I am? How could you say something so crazy?" David, on the other hand, was wide-eyed at God's choice to make him king, but he accepted the new identity. He was *surprised* by what God said, but he didn't *doubt* it. Security and insecurity both begin with the voice we choose believe. The voice we believe becomes the voice we obey—whether people's voice or God's voice—and the voice to which we ultimately secure our identity.

> Insecurity emerges when we believe the voices that diminish our value in comparison to others.

The toxic voices and circumstances of my childhood led me to do the very thing Saul did—I viewed myself through other people's eyes. Saul believed the voices that told him he was from the least clan of the smallest tribe. I believed my mother's voice when she said I was a mistake. But if I was a mistake and didn't deserve love and attention, who *did* deserve it? And how could I be like them?

This is how comparison seeps in: we focus on others who have what we want and try to figure out how we can become like them to get it. I mentioned that prior to social media, I didn't think about what people in other places were up to. But the people in my everyday life? Believe me, I noticed them. As early as elementary school, I paid attention to the popular girls—the girls who had the most friends, were most adored by teachers, and wore the cutest clothes and had ribbons in their hair. I wanted to be like them. Better yet, I wanted to be *liked* as they were liked. Comparing myself to them gave me something concrete to measure myself against, something tangible to shoot toward. I reasoned that if I acted like them, talked like them, and dressed like them, perhaps then I would be accepted like them and *matter* like them.

Maybe you can relate. You work hard to be like someone else simply to be liked. You work hard to be something other than what you are because you feel like you don't measure up. Like Saul, you compare yourself to others and are incredulous when someone thinks highly of you. If something good happens, you doubt that it was intended for you, as if the blessing was someone else's and you somehow got in the way.

The truth about insecurity is that, like any storm, it begins as a drop of rain. At some point in life, you heard a voice that questioned something about your identity. A parent questioned your intellect, a friend questioned your career choice, a TV commercial caused you to question your appearance. They were just passing statements, but with repetition like raindrops, they became a storm that caused you to view yourself negatively through the eyes of other people.

Maybe your mother said, "You're just like your father. A no-good deadbeat."

Maybe your wife said, "Why can't you be like John? He makes enough so Sally can stay home, but *I* make more than *you*!"

Maybe a friend said, "Well, you know, we're just small-town folk. We can never do anything big in life."

Maybe a teacher said, "I love you to death, sweetie, but you're no genius." That last one was said to me by my eleventh-grade chemistry teacher. It stung so bad I remember every detail of that moment, including the black-and-beige-striped polo shirt he wore and how my throat tightened as I fought back tears.

My chemistry teacher's words changed the way I saw myself that day because he made me view myself through his eyes, eyes that didn't see me the way God sees me. I didn't know it then, but allowing his perspective to distort how I viewed myself would show up years later in ways I never expected. I didn't yet understand that people don't always see you as *you* are. Sometimes people see you as *they* are.

The Cost of Insecurity

Craig Groeschel pastors a multisite church called Life.Church, one of the largest churches in the United States. A prolific author and Bible teacher, he is a respected voice in equipping people for leadership through the annual Global Leadership Summit. But not everyone recognized Craig as leadership material when he was just starting out.

Early in his journey to becoming a pastor, Craig was a bright-eyed, bushy-tailed seminary student with a fire in his belly to preach the gospel. When he was halfway through his seminary education, the day came for him to stand as a candidate for ordination in his denominational church. The committee spokesperson told him, "We've chosen not to ordain you. You don't have the gift-mix we see in most pastors. In fact, we are not sure you are called to be a pastor. But feel free to try again next year. But for now, it's a no."[4]

What did that committee not see in Craig that caused them

to overlook someone who would go on to make a historic impact for the kingdom of God? The answer is in what the committee spokesperson said. He looked Craig square in his youthfully optimistic eyes and said, "You don't have the gift-mix we see in *most pastors*." In other words, we don't believe you are called to pastor because *you're not like other pastors*; our assessment of your calling is based on *how it compares with the callings of other pastors*. We have identified the characteristics that make for a good pastor, and you don't measure up. You're missing a few over here and have some extras we haven't even heard of over there, so for now, it's a no.

What might have happened if Craig had settled into that low opinion of his gifts? What might have happened if Craig had accepted that low assessment of his calling? Perhaps he would have become successful as an insurance salesman. Perhaps he would have become successful as a personal trainer since he loves fitness. Perhaps he would have become successful as a middle school football coach. But none of these vocations would have ignited his passion the way pastoring does because he was created, equipped, and called to be a pastor.

Just as insecurity cost Saul the kingdom, it can cost us our calling. This is why the next layer of work we must do is identifying the insecure foundations we have secured our identity to.

Recall

Insecurity leads us to equate attention with worth.

Comparison changes the way you see yourself because it can cause you to see yourself through the eyes of others.

Toxic comparison diminishes us by making us small in our own eyes.

Toxic comparison filters our present identity through our past deficiencies.

Your identity is secure when you believe that what God says about you is true.

In the absence of comparison, we have nothing to be insecure about.

People's experience of you is not who you are.

Insecurity emerges when we believe the voices that diminish our value in comparison to others.

The voice we believe becomes the voice we obey.

People don't always see you as *you* are. Sometimes people see you as *they* are.

Just as insecurity cost Saul the kingdom, it can cost us our calling.

Receive

I praise you because I am fearfully and wonderfully made;
your works are wonderful,
I know that full well. (Psalm 139:14)

Before I formed you in the womb I knew you,
before you were born I set you apart;
I appointed you as a prophet to the nations. (Jeremiah 1:5)

People look at the outward appearance, but the LORD looks at the heart. (1 Samuel 16:7)

Recite

Father, I am more than what I do, what I say, how I look, what I own, or any other factor that can be discerned by flesh and blood. I am who you say I am, whether or not others agree. Help me see my identity based on how you have defined me, without concern for how others see me.

Reflect

I have often reflected on the day when my chemistry teacher discouraged me from taking advanced placement exams with his comment, "I love you to death, sweetie, but you're no genius." Saying that to me was out of character for him. Up until that moment, I was one of his best and favorite students. He regularly gave me high fives for doing well on an exam or experiment, so I couldn't help but wonder what made him say such a thing. I later learned that he had been going through a significant family challenge that had rendered him short on patience. And he was in a particularly crabby mood the day he said those words.

People don't always see you as *you* are; sometimes people see you as *they* are. Remember this the next time someone says something mean. Chances are their toxic words are an expression of their own pain.

Chapter Five

INSECURE FOUNDATIONS

Early in my career, my goal was to become a vice president of a major corporation. Where did that goal come from? Well, I worked at a satellite office of a Fortune 100 company, and I was always impressed by the vice presidents when they came to town from headquarters. These men would deliver the latest company news to a vast, captive audience of employees, and with rolled-up sleeves and no tie, they always looked confident while casually sitting on a stool. They commanded authority in an effortless, alluring way.

"That's what power looks like," I thought.

When I scanned the room, I would notice my colleagues were laser focused on the vice president. Everyone paid attention to the executive on stage, and I wanted to be him. I had no idea what the job of vice president *required*, but I wanted what it *afforded*—attention and significance.

The toxic words spoken over me by my mother and others had left me feeling like I was an unwanted mistake. In elementary school, that feeling led me to act out. I would talk back to teachers and try to make my classmates laugh to ingratiate myself with them. But the only thing that earned me was a seat in the corner and regular trips to the principal's office. When you feel insignificant, you will settle for manufactured significance.

Manufactured significance happens when you work to give people a reason to notice you—to laugh at you, fear you, admire you, or even dislike you. Anything to attract attention. I chose to manufacture significance by making myself the class clown, and I was punished for it, which is why I have a heart for young people who always get in trouble. I was one of them, and I know their behavior is often simply a search for significance.

Maybe you never had issues with approval from your parents, but kids at school singled you out to be bullied. Maybe they called you "fire head" because of your red hair, or perhaps they called you "four eyes" because of your glasses.

> When you feel insignificant, you will settle for manufactured significance.

Maybe you never had issues with approval from your classmates, but when you entered the workforce, one of your coworkers was determined to make you look foolish in meetings. They withheld crucial information and revealed it only when the rest of your colleagues were around, making you look like you hadn't done your homework.

Maybe you never had issues with approval from your coworkers, but when you go home at the end of the workday, you are always to blame for something. Your significant other demeans the way you make the bed, the way you cook, even the way you wear your hair.

In each of these situations, the behavior of others causes you to feel insignificant, and so you look for significance elsewhere.

I was fortunate to have a third-grade teacher and several sixth-grade teachers who eventually looked beyond my bad behavior to see my potential. I was also blessed to be invited to a church where a youth pastor spoke life over me, leading me to become a Christ follower at age twelve. But while learning about my unique purpose in Christ made me change my behavior, it didn't immediately fulfill my need for significance. I changed my behavior because I wanted to represent Christ well, but my newfound faith didn't radically change what I believed about myself.

I didn't instantly believe I was valuable. I still felt like I had to perform to win people's approval, and because of that, I became extremely ambitious in school. If I joined a club, I needed to be the president. If I played sports, I needed to be team captain. I can't think of anything I've done throughout my life where I was just a member and not in leadership. Whatever I did, I *needed* to be in charge because simply being a part of the team wasn't enough to meet my need for significance.

I didn't have the language for it then, but I can now see that, from a young age, my identity was secured to people's approval because my mother's approval was withheld. Approval voids get filled with approval substitutes, things that make us feel approved based on how others respond to them:

The positive way a parent responds to the As on their
child's report card makes the child feel approved.
The positive way a student-athlete's classmates respond to

them being captain of the basketball team makes the student feel approved.

The positive way a teacher responds to a drawing they see a student working on in art class makes the student-artist feel approved.

While children are susceptible to this danger, adults are vulnerable to it as well. I believe this is why Jesus makes a connection between loving others and loving oneself: "'Love the Lord your God with all your heart and with all your soul and with all your mind.' This is the first and greatest commandment. And the second is like it: 'Love your neighbor as yourself.' All the Law and the Prophets hang on these two commandments" (Matthew 22:37–40).

It is through loving my neighbor *as myself* that my neighbor experiences God's love.

This is how a parent is supposed to love a child.

This is how a husband is supposed to love a wife.

This is how a stranger is supposed to love another stranger.

But how do you love your neighbor *as yourself* if you don't love yourself? How do you model the type of love that *adds* to others if you view yourself as *deficient*? If your self-love quotient is negative, you can't give someone what you lack. Toxic comparison decreases your capacity to love yourself because it measures your perceived liabilities against someone else's assets. When this happens, you become unable to love your neighbor as yourself because you don't love yourself.

> Approval voids get filled with approval substitutes.

Five Insecure Foundations

One of my favorite New Testament stories is recorded in Acts 27. The apostle Paul is a prisoner on a ship headed for Rome when the ship is caught in a tumultuous storm that puts everyone's life in danger. The crew drops four anchors to secure the ship, but the wind and waves continue to batter it so badly that the crewmen fear for their lives and seek to secretly escape in a lifeboat in the dark of night. As they lower the lifeboat, Paul gives this prophetic warning to the soldiers guarding him: "Unless these men stay with the ship, you cannot be saved" (Acts 27:31).

Put a pin in this story for a moment and think about something. The crew was afraid because the storm was so violent and turbulent that they decided to jump ship for a lifeboat. But remember that the ship was secured because it had four anchors stabilizing it. The lifeboat, on the other hand, was flimsy and not secured at all. How could these expert mariners think a tiny lifeboat was safer than the ship itself? I've read this story many times, and the conclusion I consistently come to is that perhaps someone they trusted, someone with influence, suggested escaping in the lifeboat. While a panicked situation can make you listen to just about anybody, usually you listen to the person who seems most credible, even if you don't know them. Maybe someone the crew trusted and looked up to said something that convinced them to sneak away in the lifeboat.

Notice the voices you listen to. Sometimes we secure our identity to insecure foundations because a trusted voice led us to think it was the safest choice. Sometimes we jump the ship of God's truth about us for the lifeboat of toxic lies because we value another person's opinion more than God's.

There are an unlimited number of insecure foundations we might attach our identity to, but five stand out as most common: academic credentials, position, vocation, marital status, and appearance.

Academic Credentials

Many of us are taught from a young age that our grades matter. And they not only matter, they often determine whether we are approved of or punished by the people who mean the most to us. Earning As can unlock hugs, high fives, and dinner at our favorite restaurant. Receiving Cs and below has the power to unlock disappointment, critical words, and isolation in our bedroom without dinner.

The Centers for Disease Control and Prevention recently published a Youth Risk Behavior Surveillance System that identified suicide as the second leading cause of death for young people ages fourteen to eighteen. When suicidal ideation was overlaid with academic performance, the study found that students who had higher grades were less likely to report suicidal ideation than students with lower grades.[5] Although the study was careful not to conclude causality, it doesn't take much to imagine that the parental rejection that tends to accompany lower grades could lead children who have secured their identity to their parents' approval to believe bad *grades* make them a bad *person*.

My report cards in elementary school consisted of Ss (satisfactory) for my academic subjects and Ns (not satisfactory) for my conduct and citizenship. I can recall the way my mother's face contorted as her eyes skimmed my report card. She smiled as she read down the rows of Ss, but her smile became a frown when her eyes landed on the Ns. She inevitably glared at me and shook her head and then instructed me to go to my room. Even though I noted how her eyes twinkled when she saw the Ss, my little heart broke as her disapproval settled on me. However, things changed when I reached fourth grade. That's when, after I misbehaved, my teacher pulled me out of the classroom and said something that changed my life. Up until that point, I had been sent into the hall alone when I misbehaved.

"Nona," she asked, "why are you always trying to make people laugh at you?"

"I don't know," I said.

"You know, you are such a smart girl. You are better than that."

I was stunned. I had been bracing for punishment.

"I'll tell you what," she said. "I bet if you tried a little, you could make all As and get a good grade in conduct too."

"You think so?" I asked.

"I know so," she responded with a smile. "I'm here to help you, Nona. You have a lot of potential. You're already a leader."

Her words moved me so deeply that I remembered them decades later when my own son was considered disruptive for his brand of leadership. Knowing how important it had been for me to be seen as a leader shaped how I responded to my child.

When she took me back into the classroom, I was a different child. My teacher had just told me she believed in me. I felt so special, and I didn't want to let her down. From that day forward, I was determined to live *up* to her expectations. As a result, I made all As in her class for the first time ever—in academics *and* in conduct.

I'll never forget the first time I brought my report card home that year and watched as my mom smiled bigger and bigger as she read each row. She called her friends and bragged about my grades. She took me to Olive Garden and let me order fettuccine alfredo. That feeling of validation and worth convinced my heart that academic performance was a means to win approval. From that time on, I turned my behavior around. I did the work and became a star student. I graduated from high school near the top of my class and attended the University of Florida on a full scholarship. I made the dean's list and president's list semester after semester. I graduated with my bachelor's degree, then my master of business administration. I began to eye a PhD because I believed that being Dr. Nona Jones would bring more prestige and honor in the eyes of others.

Earning academic credentials is a wonderful way to deepen our knowledge and expertise in the area of our purpose or passion. But when the pursuit of academic credentials *becomes* our purpose and passion, we have secured our identity to an insecure foundation. For one thing, not all academic credentials are equally esteemed. An MBA from Southern New Hampshire University isn't as impressive as one from the Wharton School. A doctorate from Nowheresville Theological Seminary (made that up) would not elicit the same oohs and aahs as one from Yale Divinity School. And even if you have a degree from Wharton or Yale, while that may impress some people, it doesn't guarantee peace, joy, and prosperity.

We are more than the degrees we earn.

We are more than the degrees we earn. But when voices that matter to us convince us otherwise, we will secure our identity to the insecure foundation of academic credentials in hopes of winning their approval.

Position

Organizational hierarchy is designed to provide clarity about lines of accountability. If you're the manager at Dollar General, a director at Allstate, president of the Junior League, or chief usher at your church, you're the one in charge.

Most organizations use a tool called an organizational chart to depict who reports to whom so we know who is ultimately responsible for what. But the hierarchies don't only clarify accountability, they also illustrate who has the most power. The person at the top speaks for the organization, club, or team. They can reverse a decision made at a lower level. Because of this, when people join a company, organization, or ministry, one of the first things they learn is who is at the top.

I've been in countless meetings where the team filtered options through what they thought would be most appealing to the person at the top. None of us had spoken with the person to confirm that assumption; we simply based our thinking on what we knew about the leader's past actions and words. That alone was enough to create psychological constraints on the team as we worked to answer the question, What would the boss want? If you're not careful, after sitting in enough of these types of meetings, you'll secure your own identity to the insecure foundation of a position at the top of a hierarchy.

I mentioned earlier that my insecurity led me to pursue leadership positions because I desired the approval I thought they would bring me. I thought being the one in charge would validate me as important and worthy. Let's face it, prestigious awards like the EY Entrepreneur of the Year or the *Fortune* 40 Under 40 are rarely given to people in the middle of organizations. They are typically reserved for people at or near the top.

Those of us who wrestle with insecurity often pursue leadership positions because we want to distinguish ourselves as worthy of recognition. Many of the most renowned CEOs admit that childhood rejection created the ambition that fueled their ascent to leadership. Jeff Bezos, former CEO of Amazon, and Steve Jobs, former CEO of Apple, are just two examples. Both men were estranged from their biological fathers and grappled with rejection for years.

As with academic credentials, respected positions are fine when they align with our purpose and passion. But when achieving a prestigious position determines our worth, we're in trouble. Securing our identity to a certain title on our résumé is dangerous. In fact, many people who occupy influential roles report falling into depression after retirement because the *position* gave their life meaning instead of their *life* giving meaning to the position.

Vocation

"What do you want to be when you grow up?" It's a question I was asked as a child, and I'm sure you were asked it too. It is also one of the *worst* questions to ask a child, for two reasons.

First, children have a career vocabulary of maybe three vocations: superhero, ambulance driver, and basketball player. As we grow older, our career vocabulary expands, but only to include vocations to which we are exposed. There are thousands of vocations we never even become aware of, so our answer to that question is always limited. In April 2017, after God told me to resign from a job I loved, had someone asked me what I wanted to be, I would not have answered, "I want to be the head of faith partnerships at Facebook." Why? Because I hadn't yet heard of such a thing and would not have thought it was possible for me even if I had.

The second reason this is a horrible question to ask children is because it presumes that vocation is equal to identity. Do you hear it? When an adult asks what a child wants to *be*, they are really asking what that child wants to *do*. In other words, what you do is who you are.

I was in middle school when I learned what a medical doctor was. I didn't have a primary care physician because my mother said going to the doctor was too expensive. One day a medical doctor visited my class to discuss his work, and after listening to his talk, I decided that's what I wanted to be too. I wanted to work in a hospital and help fix people's broken bones just like he did. Imagine my surprise when I did a summer program during my freshman year of high school and met a doctor who taught college-level mathematics. For weeks I wondered why she was teaching math instead of working at a hospital because I didn't yet know that "doctoral" degrees extended beyond medicine.

When I told people I planned to become a medical doctor, they would smile and pat me on the back, offering encouragements such as, "You can do it! You're smart." I reveled in those words. I loved having people approve of my vocation and think I was smart. But what happens if you allow people's approval of your vocation to keep you on a path you no longer want to follow? Long story short, I didn't become a doctor because after I had completed two years of research with the National Institutes of Health during college, an older gentleman who had been a physician longer than my mother had been alive asked me why I wanted to be a doctor.

I looked at him with optimism and naivete and said, "I want to be a doctor so I can give my patients hope. So they can know they have an advocate in me."

He looked me straight in the eye and then gruffly snapped, "Doctors don't give people hope. We give people facts. Medicine isn't about hope; it's about cold, hard science."

That was the moment I decided medicine wasn't for me.

Contrast this with the experience of a good friend of mine.

Emanuel is brilliant. He never earned anything less than an A from elementary to high school. He was a National Merit Scholar and was clearly destined for greatness from a young age. He decided to go to law school, and of course, his family approved of his decision. He completed his undergraduate studies at Brown University and then went on to Harvard Law School. He was introduced by his family and friends as "an emerging legal star training at the prestigious Harvard Law School."

> The fumes of people's approval won't refuel you when your sense of purpose is on empty.

Within the first few months of law school, he knew he didn't enjoy law, but the thought of dropping out and doing something else was quickly discarded as an impossibility. How could he disappoint his family? He pushed through the intense program and graduated with honors. He was recruited by a high-profile law firm and began his legal career, to the pride and satisfaction of the people who mattered so much to him. But not too long into that vocation, he knew he had to quit.

Although he was brilliant at his work, it drained him. Yes,

people were impressed that he practiced law for such a prestigious law firm, but he was out of gas. The fumes of people's approval won't refuel you when your sense of purpose is on empty. He had secured his identity to becoming a high-powered lawyer because of others' approval, but the insecure foundation of his vocation couldn't energize him when the only reason he pursued it was to impress people.

To the great disappointment of his family and friends, he quit practicing law and became a firefighter. He has said many times that it was the best decision of his life because he feels fulfilled every day. While I think quitting was incredibly noble and heroic, it cost him the approval of people he cares about. Being a first responder loses its luster in many people's minds when *compared* with a high-powered attorney making six figures.

Marital Status

Marriage is considered a pinnacle of achievement for many people, especially women. Although we can argue about the role that social conditioning plays in this phenomenon, the fact is that women tend to be the first to update their relationship status on Facebook from "single" to "in a relationship." Women are often the first to post a series of photos with their "boo" (#couplegoals, #mancrushmonday) and tag him, but clicking on the boo's username usually reveals no corresponding photos of her on his profile page. Add to this the soft tyranny of women being asked, "So, when are you getting married?" while men are cautioned, "Take it slow. There are plenty of women. Don't settle too quickly."

Given these conflicting messages, women often find themselves in the discouraging position of having to defend their singleness, while men get to celebrate and embrace theirs. Is it any wonder that the moment a guy proposes, the woman posts it on Instagram? The *moment* the ring slides over the knuckle, the Facebook relationship status goes from "in a relationship" to "engaged." The notion of being wanted by someone in such a public and permanent (we hope) way is translated in our minds to the most important display of validation we could ask for. The wedding planning commences immediately, though if the bride-to-be were honest, it had already been well underway. Colors are selected, venues are visited, guest lists are prepared, and the wedding dress is purchased.

All the wedding details are measured against one standard: perfection. The day has to be perfect, and if something isn't, you can expect an emotional meltdown from the bride. But where does all this drama come from? Why do we believe a sixty-minute wedding and two-hour reception must be perfect, but treat a lifetime of marriage as an afterthought?

Unlike (most) marriages, weddings happen in full view of people's approving or disapproving eyes. The wedding is a chance for the bride and groom to curate people's perception of who they are individually and collectively. There was a time in history when only rich couples had wedding ceremonies as a means of demonstrating their wealth, but today people from all socioeconomic strata host lavish weddings, even if they have to go deep into debt to do it.

Sadly, the expensive wedding is sometimes little more than a beautiful prelude to an eventual divorce. I know several people who were together for years before marriage, then divorced within a year of their extravagant wedding. We put more pressure on ourselves to stage love for the cameras than we do to live love behind the scenes.

By itself, the desire to be married is an insecure foundation that has caused many people to commit their life to the wrong person. It usually happens because we want our parents, friends, or followers to view us as desirable. But just as we shouldn't have to manufacture significance, we shouldn't have to manufacture desirability.

When I married my husband, I wasn't trying to please someone else or make them think I was desirable. And I didn't marry him because I wanted a photo op to post on social media. It was because I wanted to build a life with a man who wasn't perfect, and he wanted to build a life with a woman who wasn't perfect. I have a hypothesis that the more perfect a couple portrays themselves to be on social media, the more vulnerable their relationship is to divorce. My hypothesis has, sadly, developed over time after seeing countless perfectly curated Instagram couples divorce "out of the blue." But no matter how lavish the ceremony or how gorgeous the photos, marriage is a union of two imperfect and broken people. When it comes to your wedding and marriage, don't exert more energy creating fiction than fixing what's broken.

When we secure our identity to the insecure foundation of marital status in the hope of winning people's approval, we only temporarily mask our dysfunction to preserve a facade and set ourselves up to eventually announce the sudden and surprising end of our "perfect" union.

Appearance

I'm going to share something here that only a handful of people know. This is me being fully transparent and vulnerable, so I hope you receive this with the grace in which I am giving it. Deep breath.

I regularly post about my one-hundred-pound weight loss and maintaining it for almost a decade because losing weight was really tough, and I want people to see my example as something that is possible for them too. As I've mentioned, I spent most of my childhood and young adulthood being overweight. After I got married, my weight climbed into the morbidly obese category. When I reached my highest weight of 276 pounds after delivering my youngest son in 2012, I felt like I could die at any moment. I was so unhealthy and miserable that I knew something had to change.

I had done fad diets many times before but decided it was time to do the one thing I hadn't done: eat right and exercise regularly. It was so hard. I wanted to give up many times in the early days, but I saw results and stuck with it, ultimately losing one hundred pounds in a little under a year. I felt great and looked great. People complimented me all the time, but there was one nagging physical flaw I wanted to address. No matter how many squats I did, my butt was flat as a pancake. Now, to a Black woman, curves are *everything*. I had been made fun of in my youth for not having a booty, so after working so hard to lose weight and build a booty naturally, only to end up with a healthy body and a flat booty, I decided to take matters into my own hands.

A procedure called the Brazilian butt lift (BBL) was made famous by the Kardashians. Although none of the Kardashians has yet admitted to having had the procedure, their unusually curvy butts have inspired many others to have it nevertheless. A BBL takes fat from various parts of your body and injects it into your butt to give it volume and shape. I decided not only to have the procedure but also to get it from the Kardashians' purported plastic surgeon. Listen to me: it was *not* cheap. My husband was against the procedure from the beginning and called it unnecessary, but he eventually supported my decision out of his love for me.

I completed all the paperwork and assessments and scheduled the procedure. As I flew to Los Angeles, I prayed for a safe surgery, but while I was praying, I heard the Lord say, "If I wanted you to have a butt, I would have given you one. I wanted to keep you humble." I shrugged my shoulders and thought, "No problem. I'll still be humble—with a butt." (Wink wink, Jesus). I know the voice of God well enough to know I should have heeded what he said and parachuted out of the plane right then. I should have saved my money and time. Alas, I did not. I was driven by my lifelong desire to have the shape I wanted.

It took several months for my body to heal after the surgery, but once it did, I loved the results. I finally felt like I no longer had to view my body as less-than because of a small butt. But guess what happened? As I returned to running and working out vigorously, my butt melted away. Seriously. Tens of thousands of dollars' worth of booty *literally* dissolved. My surgeon had warned that it could happen, but I wasn't willing to have a voluptuous but unhealthy booty, so I had started working out the moment I felt better.

It was initially discouraging to watch the back of my jeans become more and more spacious, but I couldn't help but laugh. Even now I'm cracking up writing this story. God told me he didn't give me a booty for a reason, so why did I think I could make my body obey me and not its Creator? Although my desire for a larger butt came from comparing myself with other Black women and finding myself lacking, God had made it clear that

THE SOURCES OF OUR INSECURITY

his design was best. God knew my ego couldn't handle a booty, which is why he didn't give me one. Even what we lack has purpose.

Appearance is an insecure foundation for many reasons, but one of the biggest is that people's tastes change. Did you know that Marilyn Monroe, who many people view as the very definition of beauty, wore a size twelve? While it is true that yesterday's size twelve and today's size twelve are different, her size twelve was still considered an average-sized body. Designers of today dismiss average-sized women as overweight, and this is why securing our identity to our appearance and altering our bodies to prove our worth is one of the fastest ways to insecurity.

Even what we lack has purpose.

Securing our identity to the insecure foundation of appearance makes us believe we have to wear someone else's face or body to be worthy of people's approval. But there will always be someone deemed more attractive than us, no matter how many BBLs, rhinoplasties, Botox injections, or tummy tucks we get. And apps like FaceApp and others now use augmented reality to change the way we look anyway. Approval by appearance is a losing proposition. The only way we win is to stop comparing our facts to other people's fiction.

Choose a Secure Foundation

There are many other insecure foundations to which we might attach our identity. For example, financial status, who you know or who knows you, being a mother or not being a mother, having or not having a certain number of followers on Instagram, wearing only certain brands of clothing, and so much more. Our attachment to these insecure foundations is revealed by our pride in what we own, who we know, the lifestyle we maintain, and more.

King Saul secured his identity to the insecure foundation of family prominence, leading him to tell Samuel he wasn't the right person to be king. How could a king come from the smallest clan of the smallest tribe? Like King Saul, why do you believe you are less-than when God has chosen you and called you to do great things? What might your unwillingness to take God at his word cost you? Why not choose a secure foundation instead?

For our next level of work, we're going to take a closer look at pride and the importance of activating humility to kill comparison.

Recall

When you feel insignificant, you will settle for manufactured significance.

Approval voids get filled with approval substitutes.

Toxic comparison decreases your capacity to love *yourself* because it measures your perceived liabilities against someone else's assets.

People value what we achieve only in relation to what others achieve.

Notice the voices you listen to.

We are more than the degrees we earn.

The fumes of people's approval won't refuel you when your sense of purpose is on empty.

Don't exert more energy creating fiction than fixing what's broken.

Even what we lack has purpose.

The only way we win is to stop comparing our facts to other
people's fiction.

Receive

Since you are precious and honored in my sight,
and because I love you,
I will give people in exchange for you,
nations in exchange for your life.
Do not be afraid, for I am with you;
I will bring your children from the east
and gather you from the west.
I will say to the north, "Give them up!"
and to the south, "Do not hold them back."
Bring my sons from afar
and my daughters from the ends of the earth—
everyone who is called by my name,
whom I created for my glory,
whom I formed and made. (Isaiah 43:4–7)

Recite

*Father, help me to see the insecure foundations to which I have se-
cured my identity, the things I have looked to instead of you for validation because the voices of others have caused me to believe my
value is tied to those things. Empower me to see them for what they
are—parts of me, not all of me. I ask for the grace to detach my heart
from those things so that I can attach my heart to who you say I am,
regardless of what others may say I am not.*

Reflect

Achievement has been the insecure foundation to which I have secured my identity for most of my life. I looked to my awards, recognitions, and trophies as indicators of my worth. Therefore, I felt worthless when I wasn't recognized. As God helped me see this, he steadily provided the grace I needed so I could rest in not winning, in not being the first or the best. It has been hard work to get to this point, but being able to celebrate others without feeling diminished comes with a level of joy no award or recognition has ever given me.

Chapter Six

HOW DID I GET HERE?

A few years ago, I had the pleasure of keynoting a massive church conference. Thousands and thousands of people were crammed into the cavernous auditorium; not one empty seat could be found.

I stepped onto the stage and was struck by the vastness of the space. I strained to see through the glare of the expensive stage lighting and saw a sea of eyes and smiling faces looking back at me. Not only was the church enormous in size and membership, but the pastor was a *New York Times* bestselling author and counted celebrities of all types as his close friends. However, it wasn't being on that stage but what happened an hour before that left a lasting impression.

I'm the type of speaker who enjoys participating in worship before I speak at church conferences and services. I don't hole up in a green room until it's my turn, then emerge. Before I am anything, I'm just a girl who loves God and is grateful for the privilege of getting to adore him with my brothers and sisters.

This particular day, as I was gathering my Bible and belongings in the green room to head to the auditorium for worship, the pastor's right-hand man asked if I could meet with the pastor for a moment. I figured God had given the pastor a special message for me that needed my utmost attention.

When I entered his office, the pastor stood up and greeted me with a warm and welcoming smile. He cupped my hand in both of his, and as his right-hand man closed the door, we took our seats on either side of his desk. I prepared myself to receive whatever God had spoken to him so that I could pivot my message if needed to better align with what was on his heart.

"Nona, I am so delighted to have you with us," he said. "It's such an honor."

"The honor is mine," I said. "Thank you for trusting me with this moment."

"It's so incredible to see what God is doing through you at Facebook. He has strategically positioned you, and I believe it is for a higher purpose."

I nodded in agreement and added, "Amen. I believe that too."

Then he leaned forward and asked something that startled me.

"Nona, is there anything you can do to get me verified on Instagram?"

Verification is the blue check mark badge accompanying the social media profiles of public figures and celebrities who have a widely recognizable name and are, therefore, at high risk of being impersonated for nefarious reasons. Unfortunately, some people with too much time on their hands download pictures of Beyoncé, for example, and create fake accounts using her name and likeness to get people to send them money, or they post questionable content that defames the person they are imper-sonating. Although different social platforms have different standards for verification, the common thread is that, to receive a blue check, a person must be deemed notable and their account must be authentic.

The pastor's question surprised me because, given his huge social following and bestseller status, I had assumed he was already verified.

"You should already be verified given your notoriety," I said. "Has your team applied in the app?" I asked.

"Yes," he said. "They have applied every thirty days for months but with no success. Is there anything you can do? Scammers are creating fake accounts using my name every day, and I'm worried that people are being taken advantage of."

I appreciated his concern and was about to say, "I'll see what I can do," when he said something that jolted me.

"Besides," he continued, "there are a bunch of people who have fewer followers than me who have a blue check, but I don't. It's embarrassing. I've already had bestselling books, I've been on *Good Morning America* multiple times, I host some of the largest conferences in the country. I mean, what more do I have to do to deserve a blue check mark?"

I did my best to restrain my face from expressing what I was thinking: *You have all this, and you're embarrassed because you don't have a blue check mark?*

As he continued listing the reasons why he should be verified, I realized that the pastor had equated achieving *verification* with achieving *validation*. With every book he released, every media interview he did, every conference he held, and every follower he gained, he was asking, "Am I worthy of verification *now*?"

As expansive as his ministry was and as impactful as his life had been, he had secured his identity to a blue check mark on his social profiles.

"I'm sorry to hear about your frustration," I said. "Everything is automated in the app now, but text me if you're denied the next time you apply, and I'll see if our team can take another look." Once again, he said something that floored me.

"That would be great," he said. "Once I get the blue check mark, my pastor friends will be so jealous," he said with a chuckle. Then he stood up and motioned us toward the door.

As we walked together to the auditorium and passed countless staff and volunteers who high-fived and smiled wide at their pastor, I was struck by the realization that a person could have virtually every form of affirmation and still be insecure. He had hundreds of thousands of adoring fans and followers, both online and in person. He was dressed in understated yet expensive clothes and shoes. He didn't fly commercial because he owned a private plane. He took month-long sabbaticals twice a year, during which he relaxed in luxury on private islands halfway around the world.

> Even if you're rich in possessions, securing your identity to something you don't have can leave you impoverished by insecurity.

And yet what mattered most in that moment was not the abundance he had but the one thing he didn't have. Even if you're rich in possessions, securing your identity to something you don't have can leave you impoverished by insecurity.

I have found that the most insecure people also tend to be the least likely to admit their insecurity. I would be willing to bet money that the pastor would have denied being insecure if

I'd asked him, "Why are you securing your worth to a blue check mark on Instagram?" He probably would have said something like, "I'm not attaching my worth to it. It's no big deal; it's just something I would like to have." He would have said it with a straight face despite having already acknowledged he was bothered that people with fewer followers already had a blue check mark. Clearly it *was* a big deal to him. But as long as he denied that it was a big deal, he would continue to feel an indescribable lack in his heart. You can only be set free from the brokenness you acknowledge. This is why identifying insecurity and addressing the root cause of it is so important.

Whose Approval Are You Seeking?

We've been exploring what the lives of Saul and David reveal about comparison and insecurity, but I want to include a third character as we look at the root cause of insecurity. His name is Jonathan, and although he is typically described as little more than David's best friend and sidekick, he is the hero of my personal journey to overcome insecurity. Jonathan was King Saul's son and heir to the throne of Israel. This detail is important to remember as we do the work needed to kill comparison in our lives, so I want to start with a little backstory.

We meet Jonathan in a somewhat awkward way in 1 Samuel 13. There is no mention of him being born or who his mother is; we are simply told, "Saul chose three thousand men from Israel; two thousand were with him at Mikmash and in the hill country of Bethel, and a thousand were with Jonathan at Gibeah in Benjamin. The rest of the men he sent back to their homes"

(1 Samuel 13:2). At that point, the text doesn't even specify that Jonathan is Saul's son.

Jonathan had attacked a Philistine outpost at Geba, which caused a bit of an uproar among the Philistines, so they assembled to fight Israel. As the Israelite army witnessed the size and might of the Philistine army, their courage faltered because the Philistines greatly outnumbered them. Saul and his army were waiting in Gilgal for the prophet Samuel to come and make an offering to God on their behalf, but when he didn't show up for seven days, many of Israel's soldiers ran away and hid in caves and pits out of fear.

When Saul took stock of his army, he had only a fraction of the original three thousand remaining. Seeing his men flee triggered Saul's insecurity and led him to take matters into his own hands. He wanted to restore the soldiers' faith in *him*. Although he was neither a priest nor a prophet, he decided he would make the offering to God himself. It so happened that Samuel arrived at that very moment and rebuked Saul by telling him God had appointed a new king.

People who are familiar with this story tend to view Saul as foolish and impulsive, but try to put yourself in his shoes. What would you do if you were heading into battle and thousands of soldiers suddenly abandoned you? What would you do if the spiritual reinforcements you desperately needed never showed up and your army dwindled as the hour of battle approached? What would you do if you knew you could restore your men's courage by doing something as simple as making an offering? Even though you knew you were not supposed to, would you make the offering to win the battle?

Reading this from the comfort of our favorite chair, we

might say, "Absolutely not." But when you have a front-row seat and a 360-degree view of your enemy assembling to kill you and your family, when you can see the fear in your soldiers' eyes, and when your options seem to have evaporated down to one, the choice King Saul made might make a lot more sense to you. And yet, given the same set of circumstances and what seemed to be the same singular option, Jonathan chose a different path. And this is why he's my hero.

Not only did the Philistines outnumber the Israelites, but get this: *the Israelites didn't even have any swords or spears* (1 Samuel 13:19)! I mean, come on! Could you imagine that? Even if they *did* have a massive army to match the Philistine forces, their weapons were severely inferior. The Philistines had handicapped Israel by not allowing them to have any blacksmiths. If the Israelites wanted to sharpen their farming tools, they had to pay the Philistines to do it.

When the day of battle came, not one of the six hundred Israelite soldiers who remained had a sword or spear; only Saul and Jonathan had them (1 Samuel 13:22). As you may recall from the portion of the story I told in chapter 1, this is where things get *really* interesting. "Now a detachment of Philistines had gone out to the pass at Mikmash. One day Jonathan son of Saul said to his young armor-bearer, 'Come, let's go over to the Philistine outpost on the other side.' But he did not tell his father. Saul was staying on the outskirts of Gibeah under a pomegranate tree in Migron. With him were about six hundred men" (1 Samuel 13:23–14:2).

Yeah, you read that right! While Jonathan was heading to Mikmash to fight a contingent of Philistines by himself, King Saul was sitting comfortably under a pomegranate tree far away from the Philistines with six hundred soldiers. King Saul had the manpower, but Jonathan had a different type of power. "Jonathan said to his young armor-bearer, 'Come, let's go over to the outpost of those uncircumcised men. Perhaps the Lord will act in our behalf. Nothing can hinder the Lord from saving, whether by many or by few'" (1 Samuel 14:6).

Although Saul hung back out of fear of fighting the Philistines with a small army, Jonathan courageously made his way toward the Philistines with just his armor-bearer because he believed "nothing can hinder the Lord from saving, whether by many or by few." In other words, Jonathan knew humans alone couldn't secure his victory, so whether there were many soldiers or few didn't matter. What mattered was that the Lord was with him and that the Lord could save.

> When we secure our identity to God's approval, his voice becomes the only one that matters.

Unlike his father, who hesitated to make a move unless *people* approved of it, Jonathan moved because *God* approved of it— *without people.* He wasn't concerned whether soldiers stayed or left or whether everyone had weapons; he was concerned only with the favor of God. When we secure our identity to God's approval, his voice becomes the only one that matters. Jonathan secured his identity to God's approval.

Here's what happened next: "The Philistines fell before Jonathan, and his armor-bearer followed and killed behind him. In that first attack Jonathan and his armor-bearer killed some twenty men in an area of about half an acre" (1 Samuel 14:13–14).

While King Saul consulted the faces of his soldiers to decide what to do next and allowed their fear to paralyze his faith, Jonathan consulted the voice of God to decide what to do next and allowed his faith to mobilize his fear in the direction of God's instructions.

Let's be clear about something. Jonathan no doubt had the same fears everyone else had. He could see what he was up against. What separated him from the others, including his father, is that he allowed God's voice to propel him *forward*. This is the essence of courage. Courage is not the absence of fear; courage is fear that moves us forward.

What might happen if you stopped consulting the faces of others before you acted on what God told you to do? What might happen if you no longer waited on another human being to give you the thumbs up or thumbs down before you acted on what God has already said? What might happen if the only sign you needed in order to act was the one you had asked for and received from God?

Jonathan shows us what would happen. The story doesn't end with him killing just twenty men—it gets better.

> Then panic struck the whole [Philistine] army—those in the camp and field, and those in the outposts and raiding parties—and the ground shook. It was a panic sent by God. . . .
>
> While Saul was talking to the priest, the tumult in the Philistine camp increased more and more. . . .
>
> Then Saul and all his men assembled and went to the battle. They found the Philistines in total confusion, striking each other with their swords. . . . When all the Israelites who had hidden in the hill country of Ephraim heard that the Philistines were on the run, they joined the battle in hot pursuit. So on that day the LORD saved Israel. (1 Samuel 14:15, 19–20, 22–23)

I'd say that's an impressive victory for a depleted and out-numbered army with just two swords, wouldn't you? This all happened because, unlike Saul, who waited for people to approve of him before acting, Jonathan looked to the Lord alone for approval. And as soon as he received it, he acted. Israel was saved by one man because he secured his identity to who God said he was and placed his confidence in the truth that "nothing can hinder the LORD from saving, whether by many or by few" (1 Samuel 14:6).

The Insecurity Dynamic

Although this ancient battle scene may seem disconnected from our everyday lives, I've experienced and witnessed the same insecurity dynamic many times.

As a leader of people and teams, I make a lot of decisions, some of which impact my teams as a whole and some of which impact individuals. When a decision will affect the people I lead, I do my best to check in with them and address their questions and concerns. I want them to know that even if a decision might hurt them in the short term, I have made that decision with the goal of helping them in the long term. If it will cost them budget dollars or require postponing an exciting project, I try my best to take their thoughts and feelings into account. But there is a big difference between working to bring people along *after* making a decision and needing people's approval *before* taking action.

I once had a manager who needed people's approval before taking action, and it drained the life out of me and the team. She was so afraid to fall out of favor with people that she never took big risks. If one of us suggested a big bet, something that would require a major investment of time and money on the front end but had the potential to reap a major reward, she would smile, nod, and say, "Love this! Let me think about it and circle back." From there, silence. No response. If I or a colleague brought it up in a meeting, she would change the subject or give us an excuse for why she had delayed a decision.

> When our identity foundation is secure, we look to God; when it is insecure, we look to others.

I later found out from a mutual friend that she had been put into that leadership role because she caught the eye of a senior leader who recommended her for management. She had never managed people or a budget before and was deathly afraid of making a decision that might cost her that senior leader's favor. She had secured her identity to the insecure foundation of climbing the corporate ladder. When our identity foundation is secure, we look to God; when it is insecure, we look to others.

This is true even when we have strong convictions about something. For example, you post on social media about an issue that means a lot to you. If it doesn't get enough likes within the first few minutes, you begin to doubt yourself and delete it.

You feel God calling you to become a missionary overseas, but when you share your excitement with your family and they furrow their eyebrows in disapproval, you backtrack and say, "Well, it's just something I was thinking about but probably won't do."

A major career opportunity arises that seems great on paper—more money, impressive title, bigger office—but an uneasy feeling leads you to share it with your friends and colleagues in hopes that their affirmations will cancel out your uneasy feeling so you can move ahead anyway.

Something like that happened to me once. A major career opportunity came my way, but it felt wrong from the beginning. When I prayed for clarity, God made it known almost immediately that it was not his will. The problem was that the opportunity would have considerably heightened my profile as a tech executive and entrepreneur. Even though God had said no, I still spoke with at least a dozen friends and colleagues to get their input. They all thought it was a great opportunity.

So what did I do? I forged ahead. I went through multiple rounds of interviews with various investors until something said in the final interview brought me back to myself. The conversation had been going great when one of the investors said, "So, I see you're a pastor."

"Yes, I pastor a church with my husband," I responded.

"That's an interesting combination for a tech CEO," the investor said. "I think you would need to downplay that to be successful."

"Downplay my faith?" I asked.

"Well, yeah," he said. "That would probably freak out a lot of venture capitalists, and we're going to need them to get this company to IPO."

In that moment it became clear why God had said no from the beginning. Although I would have become one of very few Black women tech CEOs, accepting the position would have increased my professional standing in the eyes of others, but it would have cost me my witness as a follower of Jesus Christ. After the interview I reflected on the investor's belief that I would have to downplay my faith to secure the venture capitalists needed to get to IPO (initial public offering). The more I thought about it, the more Jonathan's words rang in my mind: "Nothing can hinder the LORD from saving, whether by many or by few" (1 Samuel 14:6). I didn't need a venture capitalist; I needed the God who gives the power to produce wealth in the first place (Deuteronomy 8:18).

I opened my email, typed the names of the search committee members in the "To" line, and wrote "Thank You" in the subject line. In the email, I wrote, "Thank you for considering me for this incredible opportunity. It is an honor to be considered, and I hope you find the right person for this because, upon reflection, that is not me. My faith is not an accessory that I wear; it is who I am. I cannot lead a company without being led by the Lord." Several members of the committee asked me to reconsider, but my decision was final.

Maybe you have never faced the choice of pleasing people by accepting a CEO role or honoring God by turning it down, but I bet you have faced similar challenges.

Perhaps it was the time a group of parents from your child's school started gossiping about other parents, then turned to you and said, "Did you see Deborah's V-neck at the Christmas program? I mean, could it go any deeper?" While the rest of the group shook their heads and rolled their eyes in agreement, they turned to watch your reaction. A simple nod and smile was all it would have taken to fit in and be approved of by those parents, but you chose to excuse yourself from the conversation to honor God and speak ill of no one.

Or maybe your father kept pressuring you to marry your ex-boyfriend because he was a "good man." Although you love your father dearly and thrive on his approval, your ex always diminished your accomplishments and undermined your confidence.

You chose to disappoint your father because you know God created you to experience a love that heals, not hurts.

Perhaps you felt God leading you to quit your job and go into ministry full-time, but friends and family asked, "Why would you leave a sure thing for something that may fail in two months? How are you going to pay your bills?" Their questions sowed seeds of fear and doubt in your heart, but because you know the voice of God, you decided to trust him with the unknown details and go into ministry.

For my part, unlike Jonathan, who heard God's voice and obeyed without hesitation, I heard God's voice and filtered it through the opinions of others, people to whom I wanted to matter. Looking back, I realize I continued down the path of that career opportunity because I longed for others to know that wealthy, powerful people wanted and valued me. I wanted them to see me as successful. I wanted to hear them say, "Wow, that's amazing!" which to me equated to them saying, "Wow, *you're* amazing." The power of people's approval is intoxicating when you feel powerless to measure up.

Looking only at my résumé, you'd think I was one of the most secure people on earth. I've held executive roles across multiple sectors since I was twenty-three, including a visible leadership role with the world's largest social network. I've launched and led multiple successful entrepreneurial ventures. I've written bestselling books and regularly keynote major leadership conferences on multiple continents. As a Bible teacher, I travel the world preaching in multicultural contexts. Given how much I have accomplished and experienced, you may think what I am about to say is a bit strange.

Nothing I have accomplished has ever made me feel

permanently and fully secure and affirmed. No position I've held, no platform I've spoken on, and no award I've won—past or present—has made me feel secure and affirmed because there is always someone else who's "better" than me.

When I received one of *Florida Trend* magazine's 30 Under 30 Florida All Stars awards, people were more impressed by the nineteen-year-old self-made millionaire entrepreneur than they were by me, a twenty-seven-year-old utility executive. Mind you, the next youngest person on the utility company's executive team was old enough to be my mother, and I was the only African American. But in the context of achieving success at an early age, my success didn't rate as high as others' did.

Although the role I hold at Facebook has allowed for a level of prominence within the faith community, I'm reminded that there are people in the same sphere with anywhere from hundreds of thousands to millions more followers on the same social platforms, making them more influential than I am. And even though I have been blessed to speak on some incredible platforms, every time I do, another speaker inevitably introduces me to an even larger platform of which I had been unaware. That's how I know that nothing I achieve will ever be enough to make me feel secure. Achievement is an insecure foundation.

Three Questions

Evaluating our own achievements in comparison to those of others lies at the heart of insecurity. And killing comparison requires identifying the insecurity that comparison creates. This process involves asking three key questions: What do I focus on that triggers insecurity? What do I believe when my insecurity is triggered? And what do I do in response to what I believe?

What Do I Focus on That Triggers Insecurity?

One of my favorite Scripture verses says, "As he thinks in his heart, so is he" (Proverbs 23:7 NKJV). What we think about is what we focus on, and *Merriam-Webster* defines *focus* as "a center of activity, attraction, or attention."[6] In other words, our focus is where our attention goes, and as this Scripture tells us, where our attention goes determines who we are. Our focus shapes our identity.

Have you ever met someone who was in an unspoken battle of worthiness with a sibling? For the sake of illustration, let's call that person Susan.

Susan is twenty-nine and has a twenty-seven-year-old sister named Laura. Laura has always been the "desired" one. Even when they were in high school and Susan was two grades ahead of Laura, it was Laura who had a calendar full of dates with boys and meetups with friends. Laura had hair that didn't need a comb. She had a face that didn't need cleanser to stay smooth and clear of blemishes. After three hours of playing soccer, she still smelled like roses and daffodils.

> Our focus shapes our identity.

She was perfect. And Susan resented every single time someone complimented Laura. She used compliments as an occasion to say something snarky, like, "Yeah, her hair looks good, but her morning breath is horrific."

Unlike her sister, Susan had thin, wispy hair. Her face constantly broke out with acne. No matter how often she showered or how much perfume or body splash she used, a strange, sour odor seemed to overpower it. Susan spent her energy focusing on Laura's imperfections because what was right with her sister always seemed to be wrong with her. She silently cheered when something didn't turn out the way Laura hoped. Susan was so fixated on noticing anything that went wrong in Laura's life that she had difficulty enjoying her own. The only time Susan felt a momentary sense of satisfaction was when Laura experienced disappointment.

Focus is powerful. That's why the writer of Proverbs warned that our thoughts determine who we are. Our identity becomes secured to what we focus on. To understand the origins of our insecurity, we must ask ourselves, "What do I focus on that triggers insecurity?"

How often do you check social media to keep tabs on a certain someone whose semicharmed life gets better with every post?

How often do you strike up conversations about a certain someone to defame them because having someone else say "mm-hmm" makes you feel better?

How often do you scour job boards looking for a new position with a better title so you can prove "them" wrong?

Where is your focus? What do you spend time thinking about? What do you give your energy to? Whose social media do you check constantly?

Take a moment to think about and make a list of what you tend to focus on. Once you do, let's work on the next question.

What Do I Believe When My Insecurity Is Triggered?

I noted in a previous chapter that thoughts and beliefs are different because beliefs create action, whereas we don't act on every thought we have.

After years of struggling to lose weight, I had many thoughts about weight-loss strategies. I would go to sleep at night and think about waking up early to go to the gym, but when the alarm went off, I would silence it and roll over. I have maintained a one-hundred-pound weight loss since 2014, but *thinking* about losing weight isn't what enabled me to take the actions necessary to accomplish it and sustain it for years. What prompted me to act was a belief that I would lose weight if I cleaned up my diet and worked out regularly.

As I witnessed the results of my actions, my belief became stronger, and my commitment to that belief solidified into habits that have sustained me. Thoughts don't lead to action. Beliefs lead to action. Thoughts become beliefs and beliefs become actions. Insecurity results from the belief that someone else is seen by others as more valuable or worthy than you.

Although David had been anointed as Israel's next king, he didn't immediately become king. Instead, he entered Saul's service as both a musician and an armor-bearer. It was during this time that David killed the Philistine giant named Goliath. Although Saul was understandably impressed and gave David a high rank in the army, Saul wasn't prepared for what happened next.

> Now it had happened as they were coming home, when David was returning from the slaughter of the Philistine, that the women had come out of all the cities of Israel, singing and dancing, to meet King Saul, with tambourines, with joy, and with musical instruments. So the women sang as they danced, and said:
>
> "Saul has slain his thousands,
> And David his ten thousands."

Then Saul was very angry, and the saying displeased him; and he said, "They have ascribed to David ten thousands, and to me they have ascribed only thousands. Now what more can he have but the kingdom?" So Saul eyed David from that day forward. (1 Samuel 18:6–9 NKJV)

Before that moment, Saul saw David's success as something to be honored. But after people said David's conquests were greater than Saul's, what Saul previously considered worthy of *honor* became reason to *envy*. When his insecurity was triggered, Saul believed David was a threat.

Many years ago I had an unspoken competition with a friend. Let's call her Dana. Although we worked for different companies, we moved in the same professional and social circles and struck up a friendship. We were both Black women executives, which made us a rarity in those circles, so we were often asked to join the same or similar boards, speak at similar events, and join the same invitation-only civic organizations.

Everywhere I went, people constantly complimented Dana. They told me how brilliant she was and what a natural and poised leader she was. They would even ask me to support her candidacy for awards and recognitions I would have loved to receive. And I took it personally. It got to the point where I didn't want to hear about Dana's awesomeness anymore. To make matters worse, one day she snubbed me by declining my request for her help with a major event I was hosting, even though I had helped her countless times. I believed she was selfish and arrogant. Because of that belief and the way people constantly fawned over her, I eyed her suspiciously from that day forward. When Dana triggered my insecurity, I believed she was a threat.

Perhaps you can relate. What comes to mind when you ask yourself, "What do I believe when my insecurity is triggered?" Have your insecure thoughts become beliefs about people? Perhaps those beliefs show up even in what you think when you see them on social media. Go back to the list you made detailing what you focus on, and write down the beliefs behind those things and why you believe them.

What Do I Do in Response to What I Believe?

Whenever Dana's name came up, the toxic beliefs I held about her manifested through my words or my face. I often had something negative to say. If I didn't say it with my mouth, I said it with my expression. Sometimes I had to force my facial muscles not to scowl so I could hide what I thought and felt. Putting her down in an ever-so-subtle way became my method for standing taller. But putting someone down in *word* does not always diminish their *actual* standing in the eyes of others.

We see a similar dynamic in the story of Saul and David. Despite Saul's hostility toward David, we see the security of David's standing in the eyes of Jonathan in the following passage:

> Saul told his son Jonathan and all the attendants to kill David. But Jonathan had taken a great liking to David and warned him, "My father Saul is looking for a chance to kill you. Be on your guard tomorrow morning; go into hiding and stay there. I will go out and stand with my father in the field where you are. I'll speak to him about you and will tell you what I find out."
>
> *Jonathan spoke well of David* to Saul his father and said to him, "Let not the king do wrong to his servant David; he has not wronged you, and what he has done has benefited

you greatly. He took his life in his hands when he killed the Philistine. The LORD won a great victory for all Israel, and you saw it and were glad. Why then would you do wrong to an innocent man like David by killing him for no reason?" (1 Samuel 19:1–5, emphasis added)

Despite Saul's disparaging words and threats against David, Jonathan viewed David as an asset, not an adversary. When Saul ordered Jonathan and his attendants to kill David, Jonathan refused and even reminded his father that David had served him honorably. Jonathan came to David's defense because his identity was secured to God's approval, not people's approval. Although Jonathan was Saul's heir and it was *his* future kingship that was most threatened by David, Jonathan didn't see him as a threat or succumb to comparing himself with David. Instead, he loved David and defended his honor.

Several times when I said something negative about Dana, the hearers scrunched their faces in disagreement, ultimately wondering what was wrong with *me* that I had such a distorted view of *her*. Trashing others only exposes insecurity in ourselves. Even if we deny it, others can see our brokenness on display.

> Trashing others only exposes insecurity in ourselves.

Now it's your turn. Ask yourself, "What do I do in response to what I believe?" How has insecurity shaped your actions—what you say, what you do, or what you don't do? Do you avoid the person? Or do you enjoy conflict and tell them to their face, "I don't like you because you think you're better than me" (which is code for "I don't like you because *I* think you're better than me)? Or do you try to poison the minds of others with ever-so-subtle criticisms?

After considering what you focus on, what you believe, and what you do in response, you will have done the necessary prework for the next step of identifying the source of your insecurity. And once we identify the source, it will be time to confront it.

Recall

Even if you're rich in possessions, securing your identity to something you don't have can leave you impoverished by insecurity.

You can only be set free from the brokenness you acknowledge.

When we secure our identity to God's approval his voice becomes the only one that matters.

Courage is not the absence of fear; courage is fear that moves us forward.

When our identity foundation is secure, we look to God; when it is insecure, we look to others.

The power of people's approval is intoxicating when you feel powerless to measure up.

Killing comparison requires identifying the insecurity comparison creates.

Our focus shapes our identity.

Our identity becomes secured to what we focus on.

Beliefs lead to action.

Trashing others only exposes insecurity in ourselves.

Receive

Jonathan said to his young armor-bearer, "Come, let's go over to the outpost of those uncircumcised men. Perhaps the Lord will act in our behalf. Nothing can hinder the Lord from saving, whether by many or by few." (1 Samuel 14:6)

Recite

Father, show me what I have been focusing on that has allowed toxic thoughts to become toxic beliefs. Help me identify how comparison has poisoned the way I see myself and others so that I can identify the manifestation of insecurity in my life. I want to be set free once and for all and need your wisdom to open my eyes.

Reflect

As God detoxed my heart of the poisonous beliefs that comparison had created in me, I realized Dana was not my competition. I didn't win anything by her losing, and I didn't lose anything by her winning. It became one of the most freeing revelations of my life and allowed me to become her cheerleader. Instead of believing that her decision not to support me was an indictment of my worth, I was able to simply see it as the hand of God. He taught me that my destiny is never tied to someone who doesn't support me, so I have no reason to feel slighted or threatened by what they do. And neither do you.

Chapter Seven

HUMILITY:
YOUR SUPERPOWER

When I was a child, I loved watching the *G.I. Joe* cartoon. Although I didn't play with the action figures, I faithfully watched the show every afternoon. At the end of each episode, one of the G.I. Joe characters always said, "Now you know. And knowing is half the battle." I watched the show so often that I memorized that line. When I was about middle school age, I began to wonder, "If knowing is half the battle, what's the other half?" It would be years later that I discovered the answer: the other half is applying what you know.

Knowing what your insecure foundations are is important because once you know what they are, you can do something about them. Whether you have secured your identity to the insecure foundation of academic credentials, marital status, appearance, or something else, once you know that, you can begin to change the beliefs that caused you to secure your worthiness to those things in the first place. If you did that contemplative work and uncovered areas where your identity has been tethered to insecure foundations, you have won half the battle to get free from insecurity.

For many of us who struggle with insecurity, however, knowing is *more* than half the battle because we've spent so much time denying instead of knowing. I can recall multiple times when my insecurity was pointed out to me, and instead of receiving the feedback and reflecting on it, I quickly dismissed it, explained it away, or even blamed the person who pointed it out. When we respond this way, we waste precious time and energy that could be used to get free.

Embrace Your Superpower

Western culture esteems traits such as ambition and a drive to win at all costs. Because of this focus, achievement-oriented people often view humility as a weakness. Humility is usually thought of as thinking lowly of yourself or not celebrating yourself, but I believe we've gotten humility all wrong. Instead of being a weakness, humility is a superpower.

Our society celebrates and rewards the first, the best, the fastest, the prettiest, and the most talented. I've even had colleagues say, "Nona, you gotta toot your own horn 'cause no one is gonna toot it for you. They're too busy tooting their own horn to care, anyway." The idea that one shouldn't self-promote and shouldn't compete with others tends to be met with rolled eyes by hyperambitious types, but I

Toxic comparison lowers the bar.

believe this misunderstanding that one can't be both humble and ambitious has created the conditions in which insecurity-driven comparison thrives.

Early in my professional career, I joined a regional sales team meeting to support a colleague who was the vice president. He was delivering what was meant to be a motivational speech, but it struck me as a bit odd because the basis for his motivation was simply "not being losers."

"The delta between where we are and where we need to be is big," he said, "but we're not losers, and we won't settle for anything below our goal." He punctuated his words with hand chops to emphasize how serious this was. "I didn't join this team to be a loser, and I don't think you did either, so it's time to shift into high gear. And when we blow this goal out of the water, I'll make sure the other sales teams know we crushed them!"

The room erupted in applause as men and women cheered the idea of crushing their colleagues.

"And to anyone who says we should be humble and gracious winners," he continued, "I say this: humility is for losers who have no other choice. We're winners!"

The room once again exploded in applause as people jumped to their feet. But they didn't realize that their true potential was being thwarted. Instead of lifting their hearts to inspire their potential, comparison lowered their goal to simply beating the competition. Success was no longer about being the best sales team *they* could be; success was about doing just enough to beat the other team. What they didn't realize is that by setting the goal of beating the other team, they set a standard *beneath* their actual potential. And herein lies the effect of toxic comparison. Toxic comparison lowers the bar.

We are born with certain gifts, talents, and abilities that can't be purchased at Walmart. Imagine a child named Marie who has a gift for math and can calculate complex equations from an early age. Marie is a star math student and is quite advanced for her age, but one day in art class the teacher holds up a drawing by Marie's classmate Christopher and calls it a work of art. Marie looks at his drawing, then looks at her own and sees it is nothing more than some scribbles by comparison. Given Marie's desire to hear her teacher call her own drawing a work of art, she decides to try to become a better artist than Christopher. To do that, she devotes time and energy to perfecting her drawing skills, requiring her to spend less time doing math problems. As her drawing skills increase, her math grades decrease. Instead of admiring Christopher's drawing, Marie wants the affirmation he has. But in the effort to attain it, she neglects what she is truly gifted to do, which is math.

Toxic comparison devalues our gifts. Many of us are in a never-ending pursuit of accolades to prove our worth. We use things such as social media to toot our look-at-me horn to impress people and earn their attention and admiration. But we end up competing in a category in which we weren't designed to excel. As a result, we settle for manufactured significance. The attention and admiration are based only on what we *do*, not who we *are*.

Got a promotion? Post about it and watch the likes rack up.

Got the new iPhone no one else has yet? Post about it and watch the likes (and jealous comments) accumulate.

Got a new boo with washboard abs and a million-watt smile? Post about him and watch the likes go through the roof.

"Notice *me*!" the post screams.

"*I* did something great!" the post yells.

"*My* life is awesome!" the post shouts.

But behind the post is often someone who is simply searching for the dopamine drip of approval that comes with every affirming like and comment.

Yeah, you got a promotion, but you're also stressed, overwhelmed, and drinking a bottle of wine every night to cope.

Yeah, you got a new iPhone, but you also maxed out your credit card to buy it and forgot to mention that you were laid off from your job and can't pay the bill.

Yeah, you got a new boo with washboard abs and a million-watt smile, but you're also bankrolling his life since he can't hold a steady job.

Social media is a never-ending scroll of highlight reels. When we consume those highlights without balancing them against reality, we begin to believe our life is lacking in comparison. One of the most important lessons I have learned in my battle with insecurity is that *the only thing stronger than the power of toxic comparison is the healing, freeing power of humility*. Humility is a superpower because it is the supernatural ability to secure our worthiness to who God says we are, regardless of others' successes or our own failures. It is when we walk in humility that we find true and lasting security.

Defining True Humility

The apostle James said, "God resists the proud, but gives grace to the humble" (James 4:6 NKJV). Grace is God's divine power to accomplish his will through us, but if receiving God's grace requires humility and God resists the proud, what is humility and what is pride?

Humility is often believed to be having a modest or low view of oneself. In the apostle James's statement, the Greek word translated "proud" is *hyperēphanos*, which means "haughty" or "arrogant." To be arrogant is to have a sense of superiority or self-importance, a high view of oneself. The dictionary says that *humility* and *arrogance* are antonyms, or opposites of each other. So if we look at the context of James's statement, we might conclude that God resists people who have a high view of themselves but gives grace to people who have a low view of themselves. *But wait; not so fast.*

When I consider the full counsel of God's Word, I can't agree with this deduction. If it were true that God resists those who have a high view of themselves, why do so many Bible verses point out the qualities that make us special in God's eyes? Why would it say God knew us before we were formed in our mother's womb (Jeremiah 1:5), that we are fearfully and wonderfully made (Psalm 139:14), that we are unique and royal people (1 Peter 2:9)? Countless verses remind us that we are children of the Most High and heirs of the kingdom of God. Why would God say such things if he extends his grace only to those who think modestly of themselves? Why would he say such things if he wanted us to have a low view of ourselves?

While the commonly understood definitions of *humility* and *arrogance* are okay, I believe they miss something important about the nature of both traits. Having a low view of yourself does not necessarily make you humble, and having a high view of yourself does not necessarily make you arrogant. Maybe you have a low view of yourself because you disappointed your family by becoming a middle school social studies teacher rather than the medical doctor they hoped you would be. I would not say you are therefore humble. Your low view of yourself is based on others' low view of you.

Similarly, if you have a high view of yourself because you believe you are fearfully and wonderfully made, I would not say you are therefore arrogant. Your high view of yourself is based on God's high view of you.

Those with true humility derive their self-view from God, not people.

I believe that those who are most humble are those who have a high view of themselves because of who God has enabled them to be. Notice that I did not say their view is based on what God has enabled them to *do*; I said their view is based on who God has enabled them to *be*.

> Those with true humility derive their self-view from God, not people.

A familiar Scripture passage that many of us tend to speed past as if we're on the Charlotte Motor Speedway says, "There is one body, but it has many parts. But all its many parts make up one body. It is the same with Christ" (1 Corinthians 12:12 NIrV). In the eyes of people, however, the body has a hierarchy of importance.

For some people, the head is most important.

For others, it's the hands.

For still others, it's the ears or nose or mouth.

Because of this, if you're a head, you have a fan club. If you're a hand, you have a fan club. If you're an ear, nose, or mouth, you have a fan club. But what if you're the anal sphincter? *No fan club for you!* Stay with me on this for a moment.

Your anal sphincter is as crucial to your body as your

mouth, but it's at the bottom end of your digestive tract and not quite as glamorous. We take great care of our mouths. We use lip balm to keep our lips healthy and supple, and we whiten our teeth and regularly visit the dentist to ensure our gums are healthy. But we cover up our anal sphincter and don't talk about it until something goes wrong and we suddenly realize how important it is.

None of the other body parts can be what the anal sphincter is because it has a unique and necessary assignment that only it can fulfill. Yet if we assessed its importance based on how others view it, we wouldn't think it was very special.

Although I don't know who said it, this definition of *humility* deeply resonates with me: "Humility is fully occupying the lane of life that God has placed you in." In other words, humility is being so consumed with putting your unique capabilities to use in your current assignment that you have neither the time nor the energy to be concerned about anyone else's journey.

If you're a stay-at-home mother, how would you view your significance differently if you didn't compare yourself to mothers who work full-time outside the home? Imagine how your life might change if you fully occupied that assignment with gratitude for an opportunity many mothers who work outside the home would love.

If you're a writer, how would you view your significance differently if you didn't compare yourself to a bestselling author you saw on the *Today* show? Imagine how your life might change if you fully occupied that assignment with gratitude for an opportunity to write in anonymity, while that bestselling author secretly crumbles under the pressure of making their next book a bestseller.

If you're a single woman, how would you view your significance differently if you didn't compare yourself to a social media influencer whose entire brand is based on her perfect marriage, perfect children, and perfect home? Imagine how your life might change if you fully occupied that assignment with gratitude for an opportunity to fully devote your time to pleasing God, while that social media influencer lives with the fear of people finding out about their secretly failing marriage and exhaustion from snapping the perfect photos of children who don't want their picture taken.

Humility allows you to relax into who you are without diminishing yourself in comparison with anyone else.

Friend got an amazing promotion? Great for her! Perhaps she can give you tips to set you up for promotion too.

Neighbor lost twenty pounds? So cool. That's confirmation that your hard work in the gym will eventually pay off.

Younger sister getting married? What a blessing. Your singleness gives you the freedom and ability to support her in making her day amazing.

Humility views others' successes as inspiration, not competition. Which brings us back to ancient Israel and the story of Saul, David, and Jonathan.

Activating Humility

Although the conflict between Saul and David is the one that gets the headlines, the bigger conflict should have been between Jonathan and David. Saul's kingdom was established. When Saul took offense that David was winning people's hearts, it wasn't his current kingship that was threatened, but rather Jonathan's future kingship. And both Saul and Jonathan knew it.

Saul told Jonathan, "As long as the son of Jesse lives on this earth, neither you nor your kingdom will be established" (1 Samuel 20:31). Just as we hear of military coups displacing leaders around the world today, Saul feared that either David would use his favor with the people to stage a coup d'état and displace Jonathan as king, or that the people would simply bypass Jonathan as rightful heir to the throne in favor of making David king.

Although David affirmed many times that he had no interest in usurping the throne, Saul didn't believe him and wanted him killed. Yet, even in the face of David's growing popularity, Jonathan came to David's defense. The person who had the most to gain by removing David from the picture was his most ardent defender and champion. Where insecurity sees a competitor, humility sees someone to celebrate.

When David found out that King Saul planned to kill him, he told Jonathan, "Your father knows very well that I have found favor in your eyes, and he has said to himself, 'Jonathan must not know this or he will be grieved.' Yet as surely as the LORD lives and as you live, there is only a step between me and death" (1 Samuel 20:3). Jonathan *loved* David. Jonathan *celebrated* David. Jonathan *protected* David. How was he able to do such things while his father reminded him daily that David was a threat to Jonathan's future kingship?

> Your only competition is the person you were yesterday.

The answer is found in something we've already examined. When Jonathan was most vulnerable and at risk of losing his life, he advanced toward the Philistine outpost with his identity firmly secured in God, saying, "Nothing can hinder the LORD from saving, whether by many or by few" (1 Samuel 14:6). Jonathan wasn't moved by his father's fears or insecurities, nor was he moved by people's applause. Instead, Jonathan fully occupied the lane in which God had placed him as the son of the king—his *current* role, not his anticipated *future* role. The subtle distinction between the two is crucial for activating humility.

As the son of the king, Jonathan was second-in-command to his father. He wasn't in competition with anyone else for that role. It was his alone. Even if the entire world fell in love with David, that wouldn't have changed Jonathan's identity as son of the king. David's popularity didn't make Jonathan less of who he was. Jonathan activated humility by accepting the role that was his alone and by fully occupying it without comparing himself to anyone else, including David.

Why wasn't Jonathan threatened by David? Because he didn't secure his identity to being the future king. Instead, he fully occupied his *current* role as son of the king and second-in-command. If he had secured his identity to being the future king, he would have been sitting safely and comfortably under that pomegranate tree in Gibeah with his father instead of rushing to fight Philistines. If he had secured his identity to being the future king, he would have seen David as a threat. Instead, he was humble. He didn't spend his energy fighting for a role he didn't have. He spent it perfecting the role he was in. Jonathan's humility killed comparison by allowing him to fully occupy the lane that was his alone.

Some people launch podcasts and open businesses to become like someone else. Because their energy is given to the impossible task of becoming like someone else, they don't have the grace or the stamina to sustain the venture. On the other hand, when you launch a podcast or open a business because it is the natural next step in fully occupying the lane God has given you, you will not only have the grace to sustain it, you will also have the humility to celebrate others in the same field. Humility helps you to see that your only competition is the person you were yesterday.

Three Lessons for Cultivating Humility

While we can glean many insights from Jonathan's life, I see three concrete lessons that can help us activate humility in our own lives. We need to understand the differences between arrogance and confidence, competition and inspiration, and degradation and celebration.

Arrogance versus Confidence

I defined *arrogance* earlier as having a sense of superiority or self-importance. Arrogance is dangerous because it is usually due to an insecure foundation. Arrogant people feel that their physical appearance, job title, or the letters behind their name make them superior to others. Arrogant people also use their achievements as proof of their value. If you have ever met an arrogant person, you will know it because they often need to one-up you.

Conversations with arrogant people usually unfold predictably. For example, you're at a social gathering grabbing a plate of nachos and salsa at the snack table when a guy walks up and says, "Hi, I'm Larry. What's your name?"

"I'm Martha," you respond. "Nice to meet you, Larry."

"What do you do, Martha?"

"I work in banking. Commercial lending."

"Is that right? You know, I own several commercial properties."

"Oh, great."

"Yeah, they're worth millions."

"That's wonderful," you respond, wondering why he is sharing his balance sheet with you.

"Yeah, I also own two vacation homes."

"That's great," you say, feeling increasingly uncomfortable.

"You know, I only came to this party because the host is my cousin and I felt bad for missing his other parties. But I cater my parties and make sure the caviar is plentiful. I would never leave just a bowl of chips on a table. So low budget," he says.

"I'm sure he's doing his best," you say, trying to keep your eyes from rolling out of their sockets.

"Yeah, I think he's an insurance adjuster or something like that. He probably only makes enough to pay the mortgage."

"You know, Larry, it's been a pleasure," you say while backing away from the table. "I need to find a bathroom. Excuse me."

Arrogant people are in a perpetual state of comparison, searching for the smallest kernel of distinction to prove they are better than someone else. But at the root of arrogance is a deep need to be seen as valuable and to be affirmed as worthy. Arrogance stands in stark contrast to confidence.

Although arrogance is sometimes called *over*confidence, that's a misnomer. To be confident in something is to be assured of it, convinced. Despite appearances, arrogant people are *not* assured of their intrinsic worthiness or value apart from what they achieve. This is why they share the most intimate details about their life and achievements in hopes of impressing others. They seek that look of awe on listeners' faces, an awe that provides the "you matter" assurance they so desperately need. Confidence, on the other hand, is not a function of what others think, say, or do.

Jonathan's confidence was revealed when he attacked the Philistine outpost by himself. He didn't need a crowd cheering him on. He didn't need an army or chariots behind him. His faith wasn't in himself, his army, or his weapons; his faith was in the Lord. He didn't need to impress others; he simply needed to obey God. People whose confidence is rooted in God aren't afraid of looking silly if something doesn't work out, because they know God will work things out for their good (Romans 8:28) as long as they are faithful to what God has called them to do.

Arrogance seeks validation from others; confidence seeks validation from God.

Competition versus Inspiration

Although this book is about killing comparison, it's important to acknowledge that making comparisons is something human beings naturally do. We notice when someone has more or less or does better or worse than we do. In and of itself, the act of noticing the differences is not a problem. The question, then, is what you choose to *do* with that difference once you notice it.

Even one of the richest men in the world, Jeff Bezos, who has 3.8 million Instagram followers, doesn't have the most followers. Michelle Obama has almost thirteen times more followers, but even that follower count doesn't make her the most influential person in the world. With more than 1.1 billion practicing Catholics in the world, the pope is considered one of the most influential leaders in the world, possibly the most influential. But the pope doesn't have the wealth of Jeff Bezos. So no matter what you do, someone will always have more wealth, fame, or influence than you.

As I mentioned earlier, comparison leads us down one of two paths. If we notice that someone has more of what we want, we either make them our *competition* or our *inspiration*. The path we take depends on the posture of our heart.

When humble people see greatness in someone else, they are inspired and want to learn all they can in order to more fully occupy the lane God has given them. For example, if I were a gospel music artist with a humble heart, I might look at the success of someone like Tasha Cobbs Leonard, who has won a Grammy and performed on major platforms, and think, "Wow, what can I learn from her to help my voice stay healthy? What can I learn from her to make my stage presence more engaging?" Or if I had a prideful heart, I might think, "I sing better than she does! Why is everyone giving her opportunities?" A prideful heart would lead me to make her my competition; whenever she succeeds, I would feel diminished.

> When we view someone as our competition, we pin our success to their failure. But when we view them as our inspiration, we pin our success to their success.

This is what makes Jonathan such an inspiration to me. After David defeated Goliath, instead of seeing David as competition, Jonathan loved him so much that he "took off the robe he was wearing and gave it to David, along with his tunic, and even his sword, his bow and his belt" (1 Samuel 18:4). Jonathan gave David his own royal garments, armor, and weapons. Why would he do that? He did it so that David could go out and win even more battles. In humility, Jonathan chose to *invest* in David's future success instead of working to *undermine* his future success.

When we view someone as our competition, we pin our success to their failure. But when we view them as our inspiration, we pin our success to their success.

Degradation versus Celebration

When we compare ourselves with someone else and see them as our competition, it can be difficult to speak well of them. Whether it's the colleague who got the promotion we worked toward, the neighbor who bought the car we wanted, or the close friend who had her third baby while we wrestle with infertility, the temptation is to knock them down a peg. When we see their success as our failure, we feel like a loser when they win, even when there is no prize on the line. One of the clearest signs of insecurity is when we say or even think degrading things about someone's success.

Because I have done well in life, people have said of me, "She thinks she's all that." But those people had no idea what I thought of myself. If they did, they would have realized that at the times they thought I was most conceited, I was actually most insecure. When I was achieving the most, I felt like I mattered the least.

When we engage in toxic comparison, degradation is sure to follow. Degradation often takes the form of speaking ill of someone. I once had an insecure manager try to degrade me because I was outshining her. She told people I was going to be fired for not performing my job well. She told whoever would listen that I wouldn't be around long because I was underperforming, and she went so far as to say the rest of my team had been complaining about me. Her strategy might have worked if the people with whom she planted those seeds didn't know me or my work. But because they did know me, they were in disbelief and told both me and human resources what was happening. Once HR learned of her antics, instead of getting *me* fired, she got *herself* demoted. I later learned that she felt threatened by how well liked I was and thought I was going to take her job. Interestingly enough, I eventually ended up being asked to take her job.

As I have grown and matured through my own struggles with insecurity, celebrating the successes and accomplishments of those I once felt threatened by has strengthened my heart. By celebrating, I don't mean occasionally throwing out a half-hearted compliment. I don't mean praising another with false humility. I mean celebrating with enthusiasm and sincerity. Jonathan celebrated David repeatedly, which is why I believe he was able to keep his heart pure in the face of his own father trying to convince him that David was a threat. When Saul decreed that David must die, Jonathan asked, "Why should he be put to death? What has he done?" Saul's response? He hurled his spear at Jonathan (1 Samuel 20:32–33). Saul was so angry about David that he tried to kill his own son simply for defending him.

What Saul didn't know is that Jonathan's defense of David was also a defense of his own heart. By defending David's integrity, Jonathan was defending his heart against the jealous beliefs that had poisoned his father. Celebrating the success of others is necessary to kill comparison in ourselves.

Choose to Celebrate Success

Humility doesn't come naturally for most of us, and when we live in a world that rewards, affirms, and esteems the best, fastest, wealthiest, and most beautiful, we can feel pushed to pin our success to another's failure. But when we fully occupy the lane of life God has placed us in, it no longer matters what is happening in another lane. It no longer matters who is or is not celebrating us. It no longer matters whether other people see us as worthier than someone else. We can be inspired by another person's success and celebrate them because we have the confidence that comes with being the only person who can do what we do.

When your college roommate and fellow educator wins Teacher of the Year, humility leads you to celebrate their success while you continue to be the integral part of your students' lives that only you can be.

When your neighbor wins a pink Cadillac for hitting her Mary Kay sales goals, your humility leads you to celebrate her success while you continue to make the pastries and cakes that you craft so well in your bakery.

When your family throws your cousin a huge party to celebrate her release from drug rehab (for the fourth time), your humility leads you to celebrate her achievement while you thank God for keeping you from addiction in the first place.

But how do you get there? How do you detox your heart and mind from the poison of comparison to allow the superpower of humility to heal you? We'll talk about that next.

Humility is your superpower.

Instead of lifting your heart to inspire your potential, comparison lowers your goal to simply beating the competition.

Those with true humility derive their self-view from God, not people.

It is when we walk in humility that we find true and lasting security.

Toxic comparison lowers the bar.

Toxic comparison devalues our gifts when they aren't recognized by others.

Those with true humility derive their self-view from God, not people.

Humility is fully occupying the lane of life that God has placed you in.

Humility views others' successes as inspiration, not competition.

Your only competition is the person you were yesterday.

Where insecurity sees a competitor, humility sees someone to celebrate.

Humility kills comparison by allowing us to fully occupy the lane that is ours alone.

Arrogance seeks validation from others; confidence seeks validation from God.

When we view someone as our competition, we pin our success to their failure. But when we view them as our inspiration, we pin our success to their success.

Celebrating the success of others is necessary to kill comparison in ourselves.

Receive

We know that all things work together for good to those who love God, to those who are the called according to His purpose. (Romans 8:28 NKJV)

Recite

Father, show me the ways pride has led me to compare myself with others. Show me how, through comparison and trying to be like someone else, I have neglected the gifts, talents, and abilities you have given me. Show me any ways that arrogance has led me to look down on others so that I can repent and receive the forgiveness I need to start afresh. Most of all, give me the grace to walk in humility, honoring you with my life and decisions.

Reflect

When others are successful in areas I want to be successful in, it can be discouraging. What I have learned to do is to celebrate their success and ask God to confirm whether he has called me to that area or if I have called myself there. Sometimes we call ourselves to things for which we are neither gifted nor graced, but insecurity makes us believe we need to do that thing to matter. On more than one occasion, God has showed me that I called myself to something he never called me to, causing me to take a step back and shift where I put my energy.

Instead of feeling discouraged when others succeed, ask God for direction. Sometimes he is teaching you a lesson in delayed success, and sometimes success is delayed because God hasn't called you to do what you're doing. And that's okay. The key is to seek God and be led by humility.

Part Three

THE DETOX

Chapter Eight

UNFOLLOW IT

After discovering I hadn't been invited to speak at the Full Blossom Conference, I sat in my office and had an emotional meltdown. I felt angry, slighted, hurt, and vulnerable all at the same time. And I didn't like how I felt. But even more than not liking how I felt, I didn't like how *familiar* the pain felt. Some people don't mind not making an invite list, maybe because they're introverted or maybe because they have a grueling schedule that makes alone time a rare and precious gift. I am not one of those people. For as long as I can remember, I've had a high sensitivity to being left out because, for me and maybe for you, being left out is synonymous with being rejected.

I experience being left out as something like ripping a scab off a wound—the wound of being overlooked, dismissed, and not invited throughout my life. I vividly remember the times classmates didn't pick me for teams at recess. I can still feel the lump in my throat that developed when peers ignored my ideas while working on class projects in college. My heart is still tender from the times I heard about a social gathering among colleagues to which I was not invited. I took their rejection personally and began wondering what the included people had that I didn't. Rejection makes you wonder, "What's wrong with me and right with them?"

When our sense of worth is predicated on someone else's assessment of our value, *their* rejection depreciates our value in *our own* eyes. This feeling of rejection is exacerbated in a world where social media gives us front-row access to the relationships, experiences, and, yes, speaking engagements from which we were excluded.

When the day of the Full Blossom Conference came and my newsfeed was flooded with the bright and smiling faces of my friends taking photos together backstage, I felt that familiar emotional ice pick stabbing a hole in my heart—until God gave me a revelation. I heard God whisper, "Guard your eyes to guard your heart, Nona." I let the words roll around in my spirit for a little while to make sense of them. Once I understood that God was telling me to stop looking at what triggered my insecurity, I immediately felt anxious.

> Guard your eyes to guard your heart.

You see, scrolling through my various social feeds and seeing what friends and influencers were up to gave me a standard by which to compare my life.

When a friend posted a photo of herself in front of the *Mona Lisa* at the Louvre in Paris, I thought, "How awesome! I've been there and done that too."

When a friend posted a photo of his ticket stubs from

Hamilton on Broadway, I could comment, "So happy for you! Isn't that theater beautiful?" because I'd been there several times.

When a friend posted a photo of herself speaking at a small church conference, I could love the photo and cheer her on because I would be speaking to thousands the following weekend.

But when a friend shared a photo of the view from their private, overwater villa in Bora Bora, my heart dropped because they were enjoying something I'd dreamed of but not yet achieved.

When a friend shared a photo of herself backstage with Oprah, my childhood hero, my head started to hurt because I couldn't even imagine a scenario in which that would happen to me.

And when a stream of friends posted photo after photo of speaking at the major conference to which I wasn't invited, my mind raced with thoughts of inadequacy because they were chosen and I was not.

I'd heard the Lord clearly, but I didn't want to stop looking at other people's lives. I follow a relatively small number of people, and I liked seeing where they were, what they were doing, and whom they were doing it with. I enjoyed living vicariously through the experiences they shared on social media. But I was beginning to understand that what we keep before our eyes shapes the way we see our lives. When the bright light of their great experiences cast a dark shadow on my own, it hurt. Their fun, their connections, and their success were stark contrasts to the stress or mundanity I sometimes experienced while watching their joy. And the comparison left me feeling like my life wasn't good enough. Like *I* wasn't good enough. Which is yet another theme evident in the ancient story of Saul and David.

Guard Your Eyes to Guard Your Heart

I shared part of this story in chapter 6. As you might remember, when King Saul entered the gates of his kingdom after young David defeated Goliath, he was met with a pulsating crowd of people who were cheering loudly. He smiled and offered a royal wave to his adoring subjects. But something was amiss. He noticed their eyes weren't on him; they were fixed on something behind him. He glanced over his shoulder to see women tossing flower petals at David's feet. There was "singing and dancing, with joyful songs and with timbrels and lyres" (1 Samuel 18:6). But when Saul tuned his ears to the lyrics of the songs, he realized the people weren't singing about him; they were singing about David.

"Saul has slain his thousands, and David his tens of thousands," a woman bellowed while inviting the thronging crowd to join her (1 Samuel 18:7).

"David is a mighty warrior!" a man shouted exuberantly from the crowd.

"Saul has slain his thousands, and David his tens of thousands," the crowd yelled in unison while waving colorful ribbons and beating drums in praise.

Remember, this event is the turning point when Saul began seeing David as a threat (1 Samuel 18:8–9). But it wasn't the start of Saul's insecurity. Saul's insecurity had reared its head the moment the prophet Samuel told him he had been chosen king; Saul gave all the reasons why his family of origin disqualified him (1 Samuel 9:21). Saul's insecurity showed up again when God told him to destroy the Amalekites and everything they owned, but Saul instead spared the good stuff they had because he was afraid of displeasing his army, a decision that ultimately cost him the kingdom (1 Samuel 15:23). David's success didn't *create* Saul's insecurity; it simply *revealed* it. The same is true for us. Those with whom we compare ourselves don't create our insecurity; they simply reveal it.

What we keep before our eyes shapes the way we see ourselves and the people around us. In fact, a recent study conducted at UCLA found that what we *see* influences what we *hear*. Although the research cautions against making blanket statements about the link between visual and auditory perception, it makes the important observation that what we see and hear are not independent experiences; they are linked. Sometimes what we see causes selective hearing.[7]

Maybe you look in the mirror of the office bathroom and see a body you're ashamed of. When someone compliments how your coworker looks, your heart hears it as a backhanded insult of you—that she looks nice but you don't. Their compliment of her affirms your feelings of shame, so when another coworker compliments you later in the day, you half-heartedly acknowledge it but also disregard it as nothing more than nicety.

Maybe you suffered a miscarriage and are trying to be happy for your pregnant friend, but watching how people fawn over her makes you resentful. Even though these same people made dinners for your family, prayed for you, and spoke words of encouragement over you at your lowest point of grief, when they speak kind words to your pregnant friend, your heart hears, "She's pregnant and you're not."

As I reflect on what Saul heard the day he triumphantly rode back into his kingdom, I can't help but wonder if he experienced an episode of selective hearing. While some were singing about

David, could it have been just one of many songs being sung? Is it possible that others were singing songs adoring Saul, but he couldn't hear them because his eyes were fixated on David?

Although the Bible doesn't answer these questions, we do know one thing. Even though Jonathan and Saul both saw the crowd adoring David, Jonathan didn't arrive at the same conclusion Saul did about David's nature. Remember, when Saul ordered Jonathan and his attendants to kill David, Jonathan defended David, attempting to change his father's mind: "Jonathan spoke well of David to Saul his father and said to him, 'Let not the king do wrong to his servant David; he has not wronged you, and what he has done has benefited you greatly. He took his life in his hands when he killed the Philistine. The LORD won a great victory for all Israel, and you saw it and were glad. Why then would you do wrong to an innocent man like David by killing him for no reason?'" (1 Samuel 19:4–5).

When given license to take out the person who was an existential threat to his future kingship, Jonathan chose instead to remind his father why David was a gift to him and the kingdom. He chose to protect David's integrity and defend his life. Unlike his father, Jonathan did not fix his eyes on the people's *reaction* to David; his eyes were fixed on the good work the Lord was doing *through* David. This is a critical perspective shift we need to grab hold of because it is foundational for getting free from toxic comparison.

I know what I'm about to say sounds petty, but I believe this is one of those times when my honesty is the most important gift I can give, so here goes. I can't tell you how many times I've scrolled through Instagram and seen friends leaving flowery comments on other friends' posts while not providing any sort of response to mine. I'd soothe myself with the thought they'd probably missed my post. Then we'd unexpectedly run into each other later and they'd say, "That picture of your family in Hawaii was adorable! You all looked so happy!" I thought, "You mean the photo you neither liked nor commented on?" It irritated me that they saw my posts and scrolled right by without saying a word, but if a mutual friend who had more followers and a bigger platform posted a photo of a hot dog, they took time to comment, "Oh my gosh! That is the best hot dog photo I have ever seen!"

It finally occurred to me that it didn't matter whether they liked my posts. What mattered was that the encouragement I shared was received by the people who needed it. In other words, focusing on the handful of people who weren't liking my posts blinded me to the many people whose lives were being positively impacted by them.

God has used my social media as an encouragement ministry, and even though I don't have a six- or seven-figure following, I view every one of my followers as a gift, someone entrusted to me to lead with care and concern. But as long as I was obsessed with who didn't like my posts, I was missing my mission.

Comparison causes us to miss our mission. Comparison is what separated Jonathan from Saul. Jonathan ran headfirst into whatever battle God called him to fight, whether or not others approved. Saul waited on people's approval before obeying God and sometimes even disobeyed God when obeying would have cost him others' approval.

Saul confused likes with love, and we do the same when we become preoccupied with the opinions of others. I've made that mistake many times, which is why I can say with confidence that you need to guard your eyes to guard your heart. What you keep before your eyes shapes how you feel, what you think, and what you do. Someone liking what you do or wear or post or achieve doesn't equal love. Before you can receive the truth that you are already loved and approved of by God, you have to unfollow the lie that you need human approval.

This is where the rubber meets the road.

The Three-Step Detox

Not one alcoholic took a drink in hopes of becoming addicted. Their addiction grew over time and often subtly. They somehow went from having an occasional drink to needing alcohol to function. When asked to pinpoint the moment they became an alcoholic, they usually can't do it because the downward spiral was gradual and they weren't aware of the addiction until it was full blown. Toxic comparison is similar. It is a subtle poison that often sneaks into our hearts without our awareness. Just as recovery from alcohol addiction requires a rehabilitation process, recovery from toxic comparison requires a detoxification process.

The three steps I'm about to describe were the steps I took to detox my own heart from toxic comparison, but I need you to know this isn't a one-and-done type of process. It requires daily ruthless honesty to prevent the toxin from reinfecting you and causing a relapse. The sequence of each step is important because you can't take the next step without having done the work of the previous one. I'll give you an overview of the framework in this chapter, and then we'll dig deeper into each step over the next three chapters. To detox from toxic comparison, you have to recognize it, reframe it, and release it.

Recognize It: Acknowledge What You Feel, Think, and Do

Your cousin just arrived at the family reunion, and everyone is buzzing with excitement because "the big-shot executive" showed up. But you suddenly have a pit in your stomach. You were both born the same year in the same town to the same family, but she "made it," while you drive a school bus because you got pregnant at sixteen and had to drop out of school. To deal with the poison coursing through your heart, you roll your eyes and pull out your phone to act like you're busy. But out of the corner of your eye, you watch every move she makes and how everyone reacts to her.

When toxic comparison is triggered in your heart, you experience a deluge of negative thoughts and feelings that you probably try to deny, explain away, blame on someone else, or otherwise ignore. But instead of lying to yourself and saying, "I'm okay; this is no big deal," the first step to killing comparison is to recognize what is happening within you. Don't ignore or attempt to deflect what's going on inside; simply notice how you're *feeling*, what you're *thinking*, and what you're *doing* as a result.

Recognizing what you are feeling, thinking, and doing equips you to see yourself as you are. If you're the only one at the event sulking or sucking your teeth (audibly or in your head), that's important to acknowledge. If you have to exert extra energy *not* to sulk or suck your teeth and find yourself thinking things like, "Here she comes, just smile and give her a hug," acknowledge that. If you see a picture of her perfect family as you scroll through social media and feel your heart skip a beat, acknowledge that.

After you recognize your reactions (internal and external), it's time to reframe the story you are telling yourself by naming what you believe about yourself.

Reframe It: Replace Lies with Truth

When I released my book *Success from the Inside Out*, I was told that the gold standard for success as an author is to hit the *New York Times* bestseller list. I did a ton of research to try to figure out how to do it because I wanted to be validated as an author. But after the first week of sales, it didn't happen. Although it could technically have happened at any point, it never did. At the same time, three of my friends released books that ended up as number one on the bestseller lists for the *New York Times*, *Washington Post*, and *Wall Street Journal*.

As my friends made posts celebrating their achievements, I felt an old familiar urge to wallow in failure, but God spoke a loving reminder: "Nona, I gave you the book deal to make *my* name great, not yours. Thousands of people have read your story and found freedom from past trauma, and whether or not a bestseller list ever approves of you, I approve of you." Sure enough, I was flooded with messages from people who had been touched by my story of hope and redemption. Amazon reviews were mostly five stars, and the comments brought me to tears—the good kind.

While the lie said, "No one cares about your book," the truth was that God had placed my book in the hands of the people who needed it. In securing my identity to the insecure foundation of a recognition over which I had no control, I found myself anxious, discouraged, and feeling inadequate. But when

I unfollowed the lie and began securing my identity to God's approval of me and my book, I discovered the peace, joy, and satisfaction that come with resting in who God created me to be.

To detox, your thinking has to be transformed. The biblical admonition and promise is, "Do not conform to the pattern of this world, but be transformed by the renewing of your mind. Then you will be able to test and approve what God's will is—his good, pleasing and perfect will" (Romans 12:2). Detoxing from comparison requires renewing your mind because only then will you be able to discern the good, pleasing, and perfect will God has for your life. But how do you renew your mind?

Renewing your mind requires replacing the lies of toxic insecurity with truth. But I don't mean just memorizing Scriptures; I mean replacing lies with a new mindset. I have a background in public relations and am always fascinated by the PR strategy known as "issue framing." Issue framing is how PR strategists, politicians, and leaders present certain aspects of an issue to bring people to agreement.

> Renewing your mind requires replacing the lies of toxic insecurity with truth.

The power of issue framing is that, at first glance, no matter how divisive or painful the underlying issue may be, the way it's framed can unify people. The frame positively shapes the way you see a problem. As an example, when weapons of mass destruction weren't found in Iraq after the September 11 terrorist attacks, the decision to invade Iraq was reframed more broadly as the "war on terror." Few people could disagree with fighting against terrorists who were bent on destroying our country.

While reframing divisive political issues helps broaden

agreement and support, reframing your toxic comparison can help you create the conditions needed to release its poison from your heart.

Instead of seeing your brother as competition because he has a thriving business while you stock shelves at the grocery store, what if you reframed the issue to focus on the ministry God has entrusted to you in that store? To focus on how your gift of compassion and mercy is desperately needed by a coworker who is overwhelmed by supporting three children on a salary that doesn't make ends meet?

Instead of feeling inferior to the working mothers in your small group, what if you, as a stay-at-home mom, reframed the story you tell yourself about yourself? What if you focused on the immense impact your life will have in the lives of your children, their friends, and the children's ministry in which you serve at church? While working moms are doing great work professionally, you are doing great work in the home.

Instead of nursing feelings of resentment and envy when your coworker gets the promotion you've worked your butt off for, what if you reframed the story in your head? What if you unfollowed the lie that says, "You're not management material," and instead followed the truth that God may have kept you in your current role for a reason and wants you to set your heart on honoring him with excellence in that role?

Reframing gives us the power to replace lies with truth, and when we know the truth, we have the power to become free!

Release It: Unfollow Insecurity Triggers

Many years after college, I attended a college friend's birthday party and was appalled at how people used it as an occasion to compare accomplishments. It was like everyone came prepared to out-résumé each other, humblebrag style.

"I have to leave soon," Vickie said through a manufactured yawn. "My law firm is testifying before the Senate Judiciary Committee next week, and I'm the lead counsel, so I, sadly, have to do all the work."

"Ugh, I totally understand how stressful that can be," said Michelle with a dramatic eye roll and sigh. "The company I launched last year landed our first multimillion-dollar contract, and it has been a string of all-nighters to get the team ready."

"I *so* feel you!" Natalia added while shaking her head. "My husband just won his run for lieutenant governor of our state, and I need a vacation from the election."

At the time, my oldest son was still in diapers. So when my college friends all turned to me for my news, I said, "Well, I could definitely use a vacation from early morning spit-ups on my pajamas." The women looked at me with the type of condescending pity people offer to those less fortunate, then excused themselves to grab drinks. I left that event feeling so bad about myself that I resolved to make up something more exciting should I ever find myself in such a conversation again.

Some people feel good about themselves only if they can prove to others that their life is better. They are nursing the very insecurity from which we are seeking freedom, so unfollow them. Change the settings on Instagram to mute their posts, or take a break from their posts on Facebook. And if they're people you see in person, to protect your heart, limit the amount of time you spend around them.

You have to vigilantly protect your heart from anything that triggers the poison of comparison. While it would be wonderful to recognize, reframe, and release the toxic lies that lead to insecurity once and for all, the human condition makes that tricky. It is easier to notice how we don't measure up than it is to stay secured to the truth that we are approved of by God. For this reason, you need to unfollow anyone and everyone who makes you question your worth.

> It is easier to notice how we don't measure up than it is to stay secured to the truth that we are approved of by God.

What does this look like practically? For me, it looks like keeping my social media feed clear of people who exclusively post about how fabulous their life is when we know perfection isn't real and only triggers feelings of inadequacy in others. You know, people who constantly post about how perfect their life is, how rich they are, how voluptuous their booty is (hey, my booty's dissolving left a wound), or how their spouse is the human form of heavenly nectar (never a disagreement? Really?). I also stay away from events and gatherings that exist only to auction people's worth to the lowest bidder, events where people do their best to upstage each other. Some social gatherings fit that bill.

Freedom from Insecurity

Recognize. Reframe. Release. This is a cyclical process that, when implemented consistently, will release you from the power of insecurity. But recognizing insecurity is a crucial first step. Insecurity thrives when it is unrecognized. It grows when it is unnamed. It strengthens when it is allowed to remain. The next chapter will take us deeper into the act of noticing and naming insecurity because we can't defeat an enemy we haven't identified.

Recall

Guard your eyes to guard your heart.

Rejection makes you wonder, "What's wrong with me and right with them?"

What we keep before our eyes shapes the way we see ourselves and the people around us.

What we see causes selective hearing.

Saul confused likes with love.

Recognizing what you are feeling, thinking, and doing equips you to see yourself as you are.

Renewing your mind requires replacing the lies of toxic insecurity with truth.

It is easier to notice how we don't measure up than it is to stay secured to the truth that we are approved of by God.

Insecurity thrives when it is unrecognized. It grows when it is unnamed. It strengthens when it is allowed to remain.

Receive

Create in me a pure heart, O God,
and renew a steadfast spirit within me.
Do not cast me from your presence
or take your Holy Spirit from me.

Restore to me the joy of your salvation
and grant me a willing spirit, to sustain me. (Psalm 51:10–12)

Recite

Father, show me the people and situations I have kept before my eyes even though they diminish my sense of worth. Show me everything that has caused me to doubt that the assignment you have me in right now is good enough. Help me celebrate the good you do in others' lives and the sovereign way you orchestrate my life. Help me to know that the blessings and the disappointments both serve a purpose in my life. I find my rest in you.

Reflect

As I mentioned, one of the strategies I use to stay secured to who God says I am is unfollowing people whose posts on social media trigger toxic comparison. I am also mindful to use the tools social media provides to uplift others and not celebrate myself. I rarely post any news about my life or recognitions I have received because I take seriously my mission of encouraging and healing. Although I'm not perfect, I try to post only that which inspires, equips, empowers, and brings joy. I don't post pictures with celebrities I know or meet because I never want someone to look at my social feed and come away feeling worse about themselves or their life. It's why I share my before-and-after weight-loss pictures—so people can see it's a journey, not a destination. Commit to being for others what you wish others would be for you.

Chapter Nine

RECOGNIZE IT

I really believe in what you're doing and want to find a way to work together," I told her.

"Wow, this is cool!" she said. "Let's do it. Has Facebook ever done this kind of partnership in the faith tech space before?"

Amanda was CEO of a technology company that built apps and platforms for churches. Before I had even contacted her, I had worked for months to lay the groundwork for a partnership with her company as part of my work to better serve people of faith across our apps.

"No, you would be the first," I responded. "My hope is that we can announce this at our upcoming developer conference in a couple months. If it works out, I would love to have you there for the announcement."

When I joined Facebook to build its strategy to support communities of faith around the world, I immediately made a list of the top faith tech companies I wanted to partner with. Amanda's company was one of them. As soon as I saw an opportunity to work together on a project, I began sharing her company's name internally. No one had heard of it, but after I spent a few months pushing the idea, colleagues gave me the green light to talk with her about a potential partnership.

I flew out to her headquarters, where we talked for a few hours about the possibilities, and then a team of engineers from both our companies got to work. I felt a huge sense of accomplishment after many months of effort. When the feature started beta testing and preliminary results looked promising, it was decided to announce the partnership at our developer's conference. I was over the moon. The event had never prominently featured a faith technology company or partnership. It was historic.

As the day of the event approached, I ended up having to speak at a conference out of the country, so I reached out to Amanda and told her I wouldn't be there but that I would be cheering for her from across the pond. When the day of the summit came, I beamed as Amanda and her company were recognized from the stage. Later that night, I opened my Instagram and saw a photo of Amanda and her team at the developer conference at the top of my newsfeed. Their faces were radiant with excitement, and my heart felt light—until I read the caption: "So cool to have Facebook announce their partnership with our company today! Not sure who made it happen, but we're excited about the future!"

I read the caption several times, trying to decipher what "not sure who made it happen" could mean. I thought the fact that Amanda and I had spent months working together would have made "who made it happen" pretty obvious. I clicked on Amanda's username and scrolled through the images in her gallery. She had several photos with tech executives from various companies, and she always said who they were and what they did to emphasize their significance in the industry. Her posts typically said something like, "Thank you [insert tech exec's handle] for such a rich discussion about the future of technology for faith! If you aren't following [insert tech exec's handle], you need to!"

Seeing those posts triggered something in me. What was it that made her feel an association with *them* was more deserving of a tag and recognition than an association with *me*? As I took it all in, an old, familiar toxin coursed through my heart. The talk track in my mind said: "Why would she post about them and not me? She clearly likes to post about the important people she knows. Am I unimportant? How could she not know who made the partnership happen, when I spent so many hours with her? Never mind. It's fine. It's no big deal. Just move on, Nona. You did your job and that's all that matters."

> Dulling the pain is not the same as removing the poison.

I had never expected her to publicly thank me for the work I had done. I was honored to do it, so seeing it come to fruition was reward enough. What I *didn't* expect was for her to erase my role in it entirely. While my toxic thoughts helped me temporarily dull the pain in my heart, dulling the pain is not the same as removing the poison. As the days went by, the poison circulating in my system continued to affect the way I saw myself and others. I was angry and irritable. I even questioned my value as a professional.

Have you ever been there?

Maybe you found out via a photo on Facebook that a group of women from your small group got together for dinner without you. Thoughts of "Why wasn't I invited?" lingered in your heart for weeks afterward, eventually leading you to stop attending the group.

Or maybe your ex started seeing someone new, and even though you blocked him on your main Instagram, you use your "finsta" (fake Instagram account; yeah, it's a thing) to keep tabs on him. Seeing him enjoy a weekend at the beach with his new girlfriend fills you with "Why her and not me?" thoughts. And those thoughts eventually make you cold and withdrawn to your current partner.

Perhaps you spent all weekend making cookies and cakes for a school bake sale, but the coordinator looked disapprovingly at your misshapen cookies and crumbling cakes and said, "You know, we actually have enough for now. Why don't you just keep everything in your cooler until we run out?" You had participated only in hopes of making friends at your child's new school, but the hurt from the snub eventually caused you to move your child to a different school and start over.

So what can you do to stop the downward spiral? You can address the root cause by disciplining yourself to *recognize how toxic comparison shows up in your feelings, thoughts, and actions.* When you notice and name what is happening within you, you take an important first step toward freedom.

The Four Emotions We Wrestle with Most

Emotions matter. Which is why it's a shame that many of us have been taught to discount or deny how we feel, as if feelings are somehow bad or a weakness.

When we cry, we're told, "Be strong."

When we're angry, we're told, "Shake it off."

When we're sad, we're told, "Cheer up, it's not that bad."

Those who say such statements may be well-meaning, but the message is that it's not okay to feel what we are feeling. To meet others' expectations, we pretend to be strong, carefree, and cheerful.

God gave us emotions for a reason. We can pretend everything is okay and wear a fake smile to fool the world, but the one person we can't fool is ourselves. The way we feel lets us know when something is wrong, even if we don't want to acknowledge it. This is why we must learn to recognize what we feel without dismissing it or giving an Oscar-worthy performance of "okayness" that belies the hurt in our heart. How we feel shapes what we think, and once we believe our thoughts are true, our actions take us in whatever direction our beliefs lead them. Getting free from insecurity requires going to the source of our emotions. That's how to reclaim our power over our thoughts and actions.

Based on his research, psychologist Paul Ekman suggested in the 1970s that there are six basic human emotions. Today, the latest research has identified almost thirty emotions. Although I want to focus on four of those emotions, know that many other emotions may resonate with you. Giving voice to how you feel is essential to heal because you can't diagnose and treat a condition that goes unacknowledged and unnamed.

The four emotions I think toxic comparison causes us to wrestle with most are bitterness, sadness, fear, and shame. The process for addressing each one is the same. We have to recognize when we *feel* the emotion, recognize what we *think* in response to that emotion, and recognize what we *do* in response to those thoughts. In short, we need to recognize how these emotions manifest in what we feel, think, and do.

Bitterness

Bitterness is an emotional state characterized by a lingering feeling of betrayal. It accumulates over time and often manifests as resentment and disgust. When we're bitter, we feel a sense of resentment that regularly leads us to feel mistreated and disrespected.

Recognize When You Feel Bitter

Anger and bitterness are often confused, but anger is typically an episodic emotion. In other words, it is attached to a momentary circumstance and dissipates over time.

Someone cuts you off on the highway and you experience a *moment of anger*. Maybe you curse them out in a holy way: you know, calling them, "You uncircumcised Philistine!" Although the situation was frustrating, fifteen minutes later you've forgotten it and continue toward your destination while belting out "I'm Every Woman" at the top of your lungs.

Your children break a vase while playing catch in the house after you told them not to. You have a *moment of anger* that leads you to yell at them and send them to their rooms, but later that night you all play UNO together like nothing happened.

The first leg of your flight back home was delayed forty-five minutes, so after your plane makes it to the gate with only twenty minutes left to catch your next flight, you ask the passengers in front of you if you can deplane first. One of them turns and barks, "Wait your turn." Despite your mad dash across the airport, you miss your flight. You experience a *moment of anger*, but when you wake up the next morning, you are no longer envisioning the barking passenger's neck in your hands. (You might have guessed that this happened to me while returning from a preaching engagement. Go figure.)

Anger is an emotion that passes through us, so while we may recall a person or event that angered us, we don't react to unrelated situations and people in anger simply because a prior event angered us.

Unlike episodic anger, bitterness builds over time and is characterized by hostility. It takes root when we resent another person's success, even when it didn't cost us anything. When we see another person's achievement and subsequent recognition as unfair, chances are good that what we feel is bitterness. When it comes to insecurity and the toxic comparison it fosters, it usually isn't the *other person* who betrayed us but our *expectations* that betrayed us. What does this mean? Read on.

Recognize When You Think Bitter Thoughts

When we feel bitterness, we see ourselves as a victim of another person's success because it reminds us of what we haven't achieved. We feel betrayed by their success because it's what we wanted for ourselves. Every time they talk about it or post about it, and every time other people talk about or post about it, our indignation rises.

- Why did she get to marry the good brother and I ended up marrying the cheater?
- Why did he get the promotion that I worked my butt off for?
- Why is everyone liking her Instagram post?

- Why does she get the lucky break?
- How did she get the interview?
- How did he get invited to join the club?

Bitterness sees another person's success as unfair, not necessarily because they somehow cheated but because their success eclipses the expectations you had for yourself. This is how Saul's insecurity manifested the day he returned home after David defeated Goliath. As the people celebrated, he thought, "They have credited David with tens of thousands . . . but me with only thousands. What more can he get but the kingdom?" (1 Samuel 18:8). In other words, "This is so unfair!"

Thoughts of unfairness are often an indicator of bitterness. And bitterness is often expressed through words and actions that tear the other person down.

Recognize What You Do Out of Bitterness

Because bitterness views another person's success as unfair, it creates a perception of imbalance that can be rectified only by taking the other person down a peg or two. Bitterness is a zero-sum game, which means if the other person's life increases in some way, we feel ours has decreased in proportion to their increase, leading us to feel compelled to act in a way that decreases their success.

- Why did she get to marry the good brother and I ended up marrying the cheater? This is so unfair! I'm not babysitting her kids anymore just so they can have date nights together.

- Why did he get the promotion that I worked my butt off for? This is so unfair! I'm going to tell my manager about his slacking off while the rest of us worked late hours to close that deal.
- Why is everyone liking her Instagram post? This is so unfair! I'm going to report it to Instagram repeatedly until it gets taken down.

When we're trapped in bitterness, we feel we have a score to settle, and settling it requires degrading the other person until we have a higher score—even if that higher score lives only in our own mind. And yet the Bible clearly cautions us against such behavior: "See to it that no one falls short of the grace of God and that no bitter root grows up to cause trouble and defile many" (Hebrews 12:15).

If you feel compelled to reduce another person's value, chances are good that bitterness is the name of the poison coursing through your heart.

Sadness

Sadness is an emotional state characterized by feelings of sorrow or unhappiness. It often manifests as feeling discouraged, dejected, or disappointed. When we're sad, we feel a sense of loss that often leads us to cry or isolate ourselves from friends and loved ones because the pain we feel adversely affects our ability to experience joy. When sadness becomes chronic and prolonged, it can be diagnosed as clinical depression. The World Health Organization estimates that approximately 280 million people around the world live with depression.[8]

Recognize When You Feel Sad

It happened *again*. You were having a good day in the office and got the great news that the prospective client you had been working hard to snag for weeks finally accepted your proposal. It was a major deal—the largest of your career. It was cause for celebration, so you packed your things for the day and were heading out for a fun evening on the town when Jennifer ran into your office and shouted, "I did it! I booked the McPherson project! It's a $30 million deal!" Your heart immediately dropped. The McPherson project was worth ten times your deal, and as always, Jennifer was the one who closed it. She ran out of your office to tell other colleagues before she had a chance to notice the tears well up in your eyes.

You grabbed your Bible and favorite jean jacket to head to your small group meeting but stopped at the entryway mirror to practice how you would share your news with the women. "Rick and I are going to try to get pregnant one last time. We know God can work miracles and are trusting that this round of IVF is going to work." You practice the lines again until your face presents the right amount of confidence to cover your fear, then you head out. As the meeting ends, your heart rate quickens as you prepare to tell the group your news, but before you can get it out, Jamie blurts, "We're pregnant!" The women explode with shouts of joy and rush to give her exuberant hugs. It's her fourth pregnancy, and you've already had your fourth failed IVF. You force your face into a smile to restrain the tears from falling.

> Insecurity triggers sadness when we perceive a loss of self-worth.

The loss that produces sadness can be tangible or intangible. Insecurity triggers sadness when we perceive a loss of self-worth.

When Jennifer scored the deal that was bigger than your biggest deal, your heart dropped because the news crushed the sense of importance you felt.

When Jamie announced her natural pregnancy right before you shared your plans to attempt another medically supported pregnancy, her announcement overtook the attention you needed from the group to support you at a tender time.

When sadness-driven comparison blooms in us, it produces a cascade of thoughts that eventually shape how we react to the person who triggered it.

Recognize When You Think Sad Thoughts

Sadness views the proverbial glass as half empty, and irreparably so. When we're sad, a sense of hopelessness and futility often immobilizes us because our efforts don't seem to be taking us where we want to be. When toxic comparison manifests as feelings of sadness, our thoughts might look something like this:

- She always gets picked. What's the point in trying? I give up.
- I wasn't good enough. I'm never good enough.
- I can't believe this is happening again. What's wrong with me?
- No matter how hard I train, he always gets ahead of me. I just can't win.
- I'll never be as [beautiful, smart, rich, famous] as her. I'm a failure.

Because sadness creates discouragement, dejection, and disappointment, we end up thinking we're destined for continual letdowns. When toxic comparison triggers sadness within us, we need to pay attention to it because thoughts that point to doom and gloom inevitably shape how we behave.

Recognize What You Do Out of Sadness

When sadness triggers hopelessness, our actions eventually line up with the hopeless thoughts we come to believe. As a doorway to depression, sadness paralyzes us and immobilizes us by convincing us any effort we exert is pointless.

- I wasn't good enough. I'm never good enough. My little sister is getting married before me. I'm going to marry my job since nobody wants to marry me.
- No matter how hard I train, he always gets ahead of me. I just can't win. He always shows up to the triathlon and takes first place. I'm never running another race.
- I'll never be as [beautiful, smart, rich, famous] as her. I'm a failure. She doesn't even try, and she gets everything. I'm done trying.

Sadness turns us inward on ourselves. Unlike bitterness, which has a score to settle and does so by bringing the other person down a peg, sadness brings you down a peg instead. Sad people tend to use words like *always* and *never* to describe situations that may actually be *sometimes* or *rarely*. One day they look up and realize that years have gone by since they stopped working on their dream, having been paralyzed by a feeling of defeat.

Fear

Fear is an emotional state characterized by the perception that something is a threat to what you value. This could be a threat to your life, livelihood, family, or identity. Fear tends to manifest as anxiety, a state where your mind is consumed with what could go wrong regardless of how low its probability may be. When we're in fear, we feel compelled to one of three responses: fight aggressively against the perceived threat, run away from the perceived threat, or freeze and delay a response by becoming immobile.

Recognize When You Feel Fear

We tend to think of fear as an emotion we feel when we're in physical danger, but we don't need to be physically threatened to feel afraid. We feel fear when something we value is threatened.

We usually feel fear when our *lives* are threatened, but we can also feel it when our *livelihoods* are threatened. When it comes to insecurity and the toxic comparison it produces, we can feel fear because someone is a threat to our standing in the eyes of others. In this case, our fear produces jealousy.

Jealousy is the fear that someone or something will replace us in the hearts of people with whom we have a valued connection.

A wife meets her husband's new and attractive young assistant. Even though the assistant may have never done anything to indicate she is interested in her boss, the wife experiences a jealous fear that the assistant will displace her in her husband's affections.

> We feel fear when something we value is threatened.

A new family joins your church, and the wife quickly becomes a favorite Sunday school teacher. Although you've been teaching for fifteen years and people always look forward to your classes, you experience a jealous fear that people prefer her over you.

A close friend moves to a new town and tells you about the

new friends she's making at work and in her apartment complex. Even though your friendship has spanned many years and withstood many tests, you have a jealous fear that her new friends will become closer to her than you are.

The fear of being replaced is one of the most prominent manifestations of toxic comparison, and it's the reason why many people are insecure. If you can be replaced, it means you are disposable. If you are disposable, it means you don't have much value. Actors and actresses spend so much money on plastic surgery because their identity is secured to their appearance, and if their appearance ages, they know they can easily be replaced by the next up-and-coming young talent.

But you don't have to be an A-list celebrity to fear being replaced; any of us can feel disposable when our sense of approval is secured to an insecure foundation.

Recognize When You Think Fear-Filled Thoughts

Fear floods our thoughts with worry and apprehension. It creates thought patterns that quickly spiral into an emotional state known as anxiety. When we're anxious, our thoughts bound from one negative possibility to another, producing apprehension and creating even more fear. It becomes a downward spiral that feeds on itself.

- Why did Susie ask them to speak and not me? Am I irrelevant?
- I caught Dan staring at Nicole's picture on Instagram the other day. Is he going to leave me?
- She's releasing her book at the same time as me. Will anyone buy my book?

- Why did Jim get invited to dinner with the boss? Is he going to steal my promotion?

Anxiety is a struggle for many of us, me included. I often don't even realize I'm spiraling because it happens so naturally and so fast. The what-ifs of life can overtake and overwhelm my heart, which is why I memorized this biblical promise: "Be anxious for nothing, but in everything by prayer and supplication, with thanksgiving, let your requests be made known to God; and the peace of God, which surpasses all understanding, will guard your hearts and minds through Christ Jesus" (Philippians 4:6–7 NKJV).

The Bible compels us to take control of our anxious thoughts by praying to God, and in return, we will receive his peace. While this Scripture has guided me in times of anxiety, I must admit that I haven't always done what the verses instruct. Instead, perhaps like you, I have allowed my fear and anxiety to take control of my words and actions.

Recognize What You Do Out of Fear

When we are filled with the fear triggered by toxic comparison, thoughts of what could go wrong inevitably lead us to protect whatever we believe we are in danger of losing.

- Why did Susie ask them to speak and not me? I better start promoting myself.
- I caught Dan staring at Nicole's picture on Instagram the other day. I better go on a diet.
- She's releasing her book at the same time as me. I better take out a loan to hire a big-time publicist.

Fear compels a fight-or-flight response. Fear leads us either to fight for whatever we deem at risk or to run away from the threat because we believe we don't have what it takes to overcome it. Instead of trusting God to protect our marriage, our career, our dreams, and our future, we fear that it's up to *us* to protect them, which is why we become anxious.

When we're anxious, it's important to secure our identity to God and affirm as Jonathan did that "nothing can hinder the LORD from saving, whether by many or by few" (1 Samuel 14:6).

More about how to secure your identity to God soon.

Shame

The words *guilt* and *shame* are often used interchangeably, but they are very different. Guilt is the feeling of regret when you do something wrong, something you wish you could undo. Shame, on the other hand, makes you feel unworthy at the level of your identity. If you were caught in a lie, guilt would prompt you to apologize and make amends; shame would cause you to view yourself as a liar. Guilt is about what you *do*. Shame is about who you *are*.

Shame keeps your heart stuck on the wrong you did or the wrong that was done to you. Because of this, shame shapes how you see yourself. But shame also makes you believe that others view you the same way you view yourself, which makes the experience of shame all the more painful.

Recognize When You Feel Shame

While we can feel shame because we breached a personal moral code and believe we should have known better, we can also feel shame over things we didn't even do. If someone else *thinks* we did something wrong and defines us by that, we can agree with their beliefs and feel shame in response. For example, imagine you become successful and people say, "You think you're better than us." Even if you don't, the fact that they think you do can make you feel shame for your success.

When it comes to insecurity and the toxic comparison it creates, shame can take us out of the game. Shame frames another person's achievement as confirmation of our unworthiness.

Recognize When You Think Shame-Filled Thoughts

As a trauma survivor, I have spent many years working through the consequences of shame-filled thoughts. Even though I didn't cause what happened to me, I still had the sense that it was somehow my fault. I carried shame for many years because I suspected that had I been more obedient to my mother, she wouldn't have hit me and cursed me out. Had I fought harder against her boyfriend, he wouldn't have repeatedly trapped me, pinned me down, and violated me sexually.

"If I only . . ."

"Maybe if I hadn't . . ."

"Perhaps if I had . . ."

Shame lives in the hypotheticals of self-blame. It traps our thoughts in a wash, rinse, and repeat cycle of self-recrimination.

- Has Mark not proposed to me because he doesn't want to bring a fat girl like me home to his parents?
- Did I get overlooked to lead the new project because I screwed up the last one?
- Am I having trouble getting pregnant because God is punishing me for what I did before I got married?

Shame's final assessment isn't, "I lost"; shame's final assessment is, "Of course I lost. I'm a loser." And the shame in our hearts spills out through our words and our actions.

Recognize What You Do Out of Shame

Because shame shapes our identity, we often work to rectify it by winning approval from those who triggered it. We try to create a new, different identity than what our shame says we are.

- If Mark doesn't want to marry a fat girl, I'm going on a diet to lose weight and look better for him.
- Perhaps Linda will pick me to lead a project next time if I get in her good graces by taking on more work.
- Since God is punishing me, I'm going to start volunteering more at church and maybe he will forgive me someday.

Whereas those struggling with bitterness seek to settle a score with *someone else*, those struggling with shame view *themselves* as beyond repair. Shame that stems from toxic comparison convinces us that when *someone else* succeeds, it's because there is something fundamentally wrong with *us*. Therefore, shame leads us to remake ourselves in the image of the people whose opinions we care most about.

Take the Next Step

Training yourself to recognize what you feel, think, and do in response to toxic comparison will give you the language you need to name what's happening within you. Once you can name it, the next step is to reframe what you've named in accordance with God's truth.

Recall

Dulling the pain is not the same as removing the poison.

God gave us emotions for a reason.

When we feel bitterness, we see ourselves as a victim of another person's success.

Thoughts of unfairness are often an indicator of bitterness.

Bitterness is a zero-sum game.

Insecurity triggers sadness when we perceive a loss of self-worth.

We feel fear when something we value is threatened.

Fear compels a fight-or-flight response.

Shame frames another person's achievement as confirmation of our unworthiness.

Shame lives in the hypotheticals of self-blame.

Whereas those struggling with bitterness seek to settle a score with *someone else*, those struggling with shame view *themselves* as beyond repair.

Receive

A glad heart makes a cheerful face,
  but by sorrow of heart the spirit is crushed.
  (Proverbs 15:13 ESV)

Recite

Father, I am grateful for the gift of emotions. As I pray and reflect, give me wisdom and insight into what my emotions are telling me. Am I filled with bitterness, sadness, fear, or shame? Are there other emotions signaling that the poison of comparison is coursing through my heart? I incline my heart toward you, Lord, and ask you to help me see myself as I truly am so that I can become free.

Reflect

As I reflected on the emotions I experienced when I was left out of the Full Blossom Conference, I realized there wasn't just one. There was a cascade. The first thing my exclusion triggered was sadness, but that sadness soon became jealousy and a fear of irrelevance. After dwelling on my fear and allowing it to become anxiety, I then fell into the downward spiral of bitterness. But thanks be to God for the Holy Spirit! As I prayed and allowed him to work through me and show me myself, he gave me tools to turn poison into purpose. This book is the result of that gift!

Resource

This chapter has discussed some meaty topics that have implications for physical, mental, and emotional well-being. I realize that there remains a stigma in church culture about seeking help through a therapist, but take it from me: God designed us to be in community, not alone. Trained therapists offer the ministry of companionship to people who need someone who will *hear* their pain and who has the training and wisdom to *heal* their pain. If you or someone you know is struggling, know that there are resources available. Start by reaching out to Substance Abuse and Mental Health Services through their national helpline at 1–800–662-HELP (4357). The helpline provides confidential and free referrals to local treatment facilities, support groups, and community-based organizations. Callers can also order free publications and other information.

Chapter Ten

REFRAME IT

Can we climb aboard the petty bus for a moment? Many years ago, when I was in the throes of insecurity about Dana, my self-created professional nemesis, I might have done almost anything to taker her down a peg. If someone had said, "Hey, I have some information about her that will destroy her reputation in the community," as much as I love Jesus, I might have created a fake email address and anonymously sent the information to her manager. But as gratifying as the fallout may have been, I would still have been in bondage to toxic comparison because I would have felt good about myself only to the extent others felt unfavorably about her.

I chose to use the story of King Saul throughout this book because I understand him. When it comes down to it, *I was him*. Just as he commanded Jonathan and his attendants to take David out, I would have happily taken Dana out by ruining her reputation. I wanted Dana out of the picture because as long as she was around, I believed she threatened my worth in the eyes of others.

Now that I have the language for it, I know my issue with Dana was that I had secured my identity to the insecure foundation of people's approval. And those people seemed to approve of her more than me. Or so I thought.

As I was doing the internal work to address my insecurity, I felt compelled to reach out to Dana and share how much God was maturing me regarding how I viewed myself in comparison to her. As it turned out, Dana said that the same people who were celebrating *her to me* were celebrating *me to her.* The story I had believed—that people saw her as better than me—was never the case!

"It's funny how insecurity makes us think a compliment about someone else is a put-down to us," she said. "I remember being in meetings where your name would come up and people would smile widely. They loved you, girl."

"Professional success doesn't make us immune to insecurity," I responded. "I think it may actually make it worse because the more we achieve, the more we realize what we haven't achieved."

"You're absolutely right, Nona! These awards and recognitions are nice in the moment, but a week later it's like it didn't even happen. There's always another one," she said with a sigh.

We spent more than an hour talking through our experiences as professional women of color and how being "the only one" like you in a room can trigger insecurity if you let it. It can make you secure your identity to being "the only one," and when that happens, if someone else who looks like you inches their way into the room, you think your access to the room is at risk. Since you believe there can be only one of you, you feel threatened and fear being replaced. That fear (jealousy) of being replaced will lead you to behave in ways that shut and bolt the door closed behind you. For example, you might speak ill of the other person or undermine their invitation to the room by blocking a promotion, dissuading a host from inviting them to a party, or spreading rumors about them on social media. I know of several situations in which a woman broke a glass ceiling, only to allow her own fear-fueled emotions, thoughts, and actions to create a thicker glass ceiling in its place. She had the potential to open a door for others but instead did everything she could to eliminate the competition. Toxic comparison picks a fight where there is no prize.

Think about it. Even if I had "won" and managed to make people in our professional circle believe I was "better" than Dana, there would still have been someone somewhere who was "better" than me, so "beating" Dana wouldn't have won me anything. Someone will always have more money, more connections, more power, more influence, a happier marriage, a fitter body, children with better grades, or a husband with better abs (except for mine because my husband's abs are amazing, and I'm not just saying that because he's reading this as I write it). It goes on and on and on. But I had an insight during my conversation with Dana that has helped free me from insecurity: insecurity is like a game.

> Toxic comparison picks a fight where there is no prize.

Games have four key components: players, goals, rules, and challenges. When your insecurity is triggered, you and the person who triggered your insecurity become the players (even if the other person doesn't know they're a player). Your goal becomes getting ahead of them on the game board of life, and the only rule you play by is "don't lose." Challenges arise when your opponent gets ahead of you, which triggers feelings, thoughts, and actions that cause you to act out of character.

But if insecurity is like a game, what if you invited a third player to the table? The Holy Spirit. Instead of trying not to lose to the person who triggered your insecurity, what if you turned to the Holy Spirit and asked him to remind you that you can't lose since the Lord is on your side? Instead of feeling defeated when the other player gets ahead of you on the game board, what if you asked the Holy Spirit to remind you that your identity is found in God's love, not other people's likes?

When your insecurity is triggered, turn to the Holy Spirit and ask him for the power to reframe your thinking.

The Power of Reframing

"Mrs. Jones, we need to have a talk," my son's second-grade teacher said as I took a seat in the gray chair across from her desk. "Isaac is a lovely boy. He's helpful and loves to serve. But we have a problem."

"Oh boy. What did he do?" I asked as I prepared my heart for a major bomb.

"Well, whenever I give another student an instruction, Isaac takes it upon himself to repeat what I said to the student as if he's a teacher too," she explained. "Then if the student disobeys what I said, instead of telling me, Isaac will yell at the child and tell them to go to time-out. While I appreciate how he is a stickler for rules, it's become disruptive. I've told him not to do it, but he still does."

I restrained a chuckle as I imagined my sweet, chubby-cheeked baby boy telling his fellow diminutive classmates to go to time-out. "Hmm. Okay. I see," I said. "Well, Isaac definitely has a strong sense of right and wrong. When you couple that with his strong sense of duty, I can see how that could lead to a disruption. I'll speak with him about it."

"Thank you so much," she responded. "I told him that if it continues, he will have to go to the dean's office. It's undermining my leadership."

I left the classroom to meet Isaac in the lobby, where he was waiting for me. He greeted me with his usual excited smile and said, "Mommy! What did she say?" He already knew, of course, but his asking me as if he didn't made me smile on the inside.

"Well, she said you're being bossy," I said. "You're telling your classmates what to do after she gives them instructions. You shouldn't be repeating what she says as if you're a deputy teacher, Isaac. You're not."

He looked disappointed and said, "I was just trying to help."

I cupped his chin in my hands and said, "I know you were, but you can't help your teacher by undermining her leadership."

He got a twinkle in his eye and said, "But, Mommy, that's what I was trying to do. I was just trying to show leadership!"

In an instant, my little guy did something that public relations professionals, politicians, and business leaders alike have been doing for decades to increase support for their ideas. He took his teacher's assessment of insubordination and reframed it as leadership. He took his teacher's accusation of *misbehaving* in class and transformed it into an example of *contributing* to his class.

As I mentioned in chapter 8, describing a problem in a way that promotes support is known as "issue framing." It's half art and half science because the way you frame an issue depends on what will resonate most with the audience you are trying to convince.

Let's say you've created a new yogurt that you want to release into the market. Before you do, you get a group of dieticians to put their public support behind it as part of a public relations campaign. You know the dieticians pay a lot of attention to nutritional values, so while the yogurt contains 20 percent fat, you promote it to them as 80 percent fat-free. See what I did there? The truth didn't change; being 80 percent fat-free means the yogurt is (still) 20 percent fat. The truth didn't change, but the way you framed it did.

Toxic comparison is easy to recognize because it causes us to emphasize something we lack.

- Why can't my flabby arms be toned like Jenny's?
- Jason's business is thriving, while my customers are leaving left and right.
- I wish Alan would hold me the way Mark holds Sandra.

In each of these examples, the emphasis is on the lack—a lack of toned arms, a lack of customers, and a lack of intimacy. Remember, while healthy comparison causes inspiration, toxic comparison eventually causes expiration by killing our sense of hope, worth, and possibility. It emphasizes what we don't have and leads us to conclude that we are deficient as a result.

While toxic comparison emphasizes deficiency, God's truth emphasizes abundance. Here's how reframing our thinking through the truth of God would change the way we see each of these situations.

- My arms may not be as toned as Jenny's, but they allow me to pick up my children and swing them around. Thank you, God, for strong arms!
- My business may not be as profitable as Jason's right now, but every lost customer is teaching me how to do things better next time. And I will. Thank you, God, for the opportunity to learn.
- Alan may not hold me the way Mark holds Sandra, but when I was going through chemotherapy, he never once left my side. Thank you, God, for a man who shows his love through loyalty.

I did three things in reframing these scenarios. First, I acknowledged what I was thinking. If we don't acknowledge what we're thinking, the poison of comparison will continue to course through our hearts unimpeded.

Second, I took stock of the good things. Buckle your seat belt because this one is a game changer: a perceived lack is actually a disguised abundance. Scripture promises, "All things work together for good to those who love God, to those who are called according to His purpose" (Romans 8:28 NKJV). Notice, it doesn't say, "All things *feel* good"; it says, "All things work together *for* good." Those jiggly arms pick up giggly kids. That loss of revenue motivates increased faith. The missing hugs and kisses are manifested in the favorite cup of coffee Alan makes you every morning. Our lack is often simply abundance in disguise, which means we have to look for it.

> A perceived lack is actually a disguised abundance.

Finally, I reframed toxic, self-defeating thinking into an opportunity for thanksgiving. When we take the time to discover the hidden abundance in our lack, we train our hearts to celebrate sufficiency instead of grieving deficiency. As I reflect on my struggles with toxic comparison, I see a common thread. Whether it was my weight, an unspoken competition, or not being invited to the Full Blossom Conference, emphasizing my lack made me feel increasingly unworthy, which created a self-fulfilling downward spiral.

Emphasizing my lack instead of my abundance allowed lies to take root in my heart. Discovering this truth and choosing to emphasize abundance instead has been one of the most freeing exercises I have ever done. It has given me the power to reframe the toxic lies for life-giving freedom! But first I had to get honest with myself in a very painful way.

I had to admit that *I* had become the most toxic voice in my life. Not anyone else. Not the posts I saw on social media. Not the photos I saw in magazines or on television. *Me.* Yes, unkind remarks had been made to me, and, yes, those words hurt so badly that they shattered my heart. But I eventually had to ask myself, "Nona, what do you believe about yourself that is making the compliments *others* receive poisonous to *you*?" My heart had gotten to a state where what should have been neutral, like compliments of others, became toxic to me, and it's a question I invite you to ask yourself.

What do you believe about *yourself* that is making another person's success or achievement poisonous to you? What self-narrative needs to be named and reframed? Your self-narrative determines to whom and to what you secure your identity. And this is why getting free from toxic comparison requires reframing every narrative that lies to you about who you are.

- **I'M NOT SUCCESSFUL ENOUGH.** This toxic narrative makes you sensitive to others' wealth, fame, or social connections.
- **I'M NOT SMART ENOUGH.** This toxic narrative makes you sensitive to others' academic achievements.
- **I'M UNATTRACTIVE.** This toxic narrative makes you sensitive to others' physical appearance.
- **I'M UNLOVABLE.** This toxic narrative makes you sensitive to others dating, getting engaged, or getting married.
- **I'M UNWORTHY.** This toxic narrative makes you sensitive to being left out and overlooked.
- **I'M UNKNOWN.** This toxic narrative makes you sensitive to others being recognized for things you want to be known for.
- **I'M _____.** This toxic narrative makes you sensitive to _____.

The toxic self-narrative that has governed a lot of my thought life is the idea that I'm unwanted. This belief makes me sensitive to people walking away and abandoning me. As a result of this belief, I've kept some people in my life long past our relational expiration date simply because their sticking around made me feel wanted. Forget that they used me and only came around when they wanted something from me; believing I was unwanted made me susceptible to being mistreated.

Understanding the power of toxic narratives puts you in the position to reframe the lies. But how?

Three Biblical Reframers

Killing comparison was a difficult process because I didn't have a framework for how to do it. Sure, I had great books that affirmed my value in God's sight and that gave me positive affirmations to speak over myself. What I didn't have were role models and practical examples I could relate to. But as I studied the Bible, I discovered three relationships that provide excellent examples of what it means to reframe the lies of toxic comparison. They include Jonathan and David, whom we've already considered, John the Baptist and Jesus, and Paul and Apollos.

Jonathan and David

As a refresher, Jonathan's father, Saul, was king of Israel, but he became jealous of David because he feared David would replace him as king. Saul secured his identity to people's approval, and when the people seemed to approve of David more than him, Saul felt threatened.

Saul not only felt that his own kingship was threatened—he also expressed concern for Jonathan's future kingship. However, Jonathan wasn't threatened by David. Instead, Jonathan loved and celebrated David, which is the first key to reframing. Celebrating the success of others kills comparison. When David was victorious in battle, Jonathan didn't sulk or otherwise try to undermine David's favor among the people. Instead, Jonathan cheered the loudest because he knew David's success was not his failure. While the truth is that David's presence *did* put Jonathan's future kingship in jeopardy, it wasn't for the reason Saul assumed. It wasn't because *people* approved of David but because *God* did.

Jonathan celebrated David because God celebrated David. The favor in David's life was favor given by *God*. God also orchestrates the favor in the life of the person who triggers your toxic comparison. Instead of sulking because a friend got invited to join the social club you had been secretly hoping to join, what if you celebrated her and let her know you're proud of her? When other people talk behind her back and say she's stuck up, conceited, or thinks she's all that, what if you were to follow Jonathan's example and defend her?

> Jonathan celebrated David because God celebrated David.

We should celebrate others because God celebrates others.

You kill comparison when you reframe it as celebration.

John the Baptist and Jesus

John the Baptist prepared the way for Jesus. When asked to explain himself to a group of Jewish religious leaders, he said, "I am the voice of one calling in the wilderness, 'Make straight the way for the Lord'" (John 1:23). Yet he may have been surprised when all his preparation came to fruition: "The next day John was there again with two of his disciples. When he saw Jesus passing by, he said, 'Look, the Lamb of God!' When the two disciples heard him say this, they followed Jesus" (John 1:35–37). Follow me for a moment.

John had spent at least one year talking about the coming Messiah. He had built a huge following and made a name for himself. If he'd had an Instagram account, it would definitely have been blue-check verified because John the Baptist was well respected and well known. Then Jesus showed up on the scene. The one for whom John had done all that preparation. The one around whom John had built his entire ministry. And the moment John pointed out Jesus to the people he had lovingly shepherded, many left him to follow Jesus.

On an intellectual level, it makes sense, right? I mean, that's why John had spent years calling people to repent and baptizing them. But on an emotional level, wow. If I were him, I would have been a bit hurt. If I were him, I would have been a bit offended. If I were him, seeing my close friends and disciples leave my side before I could finish my thought would have kicked up some serious insecurity. But since I'm not him, the lesson I learn from his life is a powerful one.

Instead of thinking, "Wow, they've abandoned me for him," John thought, "Wow, I've been so effective in ministry, they are now ready to follow the Messiah. Mission complete." John recognized that his mission required him to build a following that would ultimately leave him to follow Jesus.

So instead of feeling angry because a young woman you mentored excelled at her job and got promoted above you, what if you reframe the situation? Instead, you could be confident that you did what you were called to do and completed your mission. Imagine the rest you will find in knowing you've given your all and that God will reward your service.

When people walk away from us, sometimes their departure simply ushers us into a new assignment. Drawing on John's example, we can reframe abandonment as reassignment. For those of us who have had parents, siblings, close friends, or colleagues walk away from us, the wound can be so deep that we struggle to see any purpose in the pain. But I have learned from experience that even that type of abandonment can birth a redemptive reassignment. It has built empathy in my heart for others who have been abandoned, creating a ministry of healing I could have never had if I hadn't experienced it myself. God is a healer of broken hearts.

Paul and Apollos

In his first letter to the church at Corinth, the apostle Paul wrote to instruct believers who were struggling in various areas of holiness. As people do, the Corinthian people had followed, liked, and shared their favorite preachers on that day's version of social media (I think it was called the grapevine). This led to division, strife, and factions among the people. Some were #TeamPaul and others were #TeamApollos. When Paul caught wind of what was happening, he didn't fan the flames of division by putting out cooler content than Apollos in hopes of winning back his fans. No, he took an entirely different approach. Paul wrote,

> Who is Apollos? Who is Paul? We are only God's servants through whom you believed the Good News. Each of us did the work the Lord gave us. I planted the seed in your hearts, and Apollos watered it, but it was God who made it grow. It's not important who does the planting, or who does the watering. What's important is that God makes the seed grow. The one who plants and the one who waters work together with the same purpose. And both will be rewarded for their own hard work. For we are both God's workers. And you are God's field. You are God's building. (1 Corinthians 3:5–9 NLT)

Every time I read this passage, I feel the pride evaporate from my heart. Paul makes sure the people understand that there is nothing special about him or Apollos beyond what God does through them; they are simply co-laborers, both of whom are used by God. This reframing serves as a reminder that no matter how special we think someone—ourselves included—may be, it is God who gives the increase.

Instead of thinking, "George is so thoughtful and loving to Laura. Why can't James be that way?" what if you reframed this thought. You might think, "James is such a gift to me because, while he may not do PDA (public displays of affection), he is never MIA (missing in action). I can always count on him to be a man of his word."

Often we wish we had what someone else has because the lawn of their life seems to be thriving, while ours seems to be dead or dying. But sometimes that's because we're so busy paying attention to their lawn that we aren't taking care of our own. We water the grass of our lives when we celebrate the good times, cultivate gratitude for our blessings, and appreciate what we have. Greener grass is simply well-watered grass.

You kill comparison when you reframe the lie that you need someone else's lawn to be happy and secure.

From Lies to Truth

I've said it before, but it bears repeating. When I struggled with insecurity, reading verses about how much God loved me wasn't enough to free me from my pain. Now I understand that was because I didn't know anything about noticing and naming the source of my insecurity, so I would simply try to fill my mind with more and more verses about worthiness. But it didn't help because my problem wasn't in my mind, it was in my heart.

Heart problems can't be fixed in our heads. So I didn't need to simply memorize more Scripture, I needed to replace the beliefs that had me bound.

The apostle James wrote, "Every good and perfect gift is from above, coming down from the Father of the heavenly lights, who does not change like shifting shadows" (James 1:17). Our heavenly Father gives good and perfect gifts. Because it is God who gives those gifts, comparing our perceived lack to someone else's abundance is misguided. Remember, what we think of as lack is simply abundance in disguise. We must reframe our perceptions from lies to truth.

> Heart problems can't be fixed in our heads.

- From: I'm not successful enough. To: I'm grateful for what I have and what I'm building.
- From: I'm not smart enough. To: I'm learning new things every day.
- From: I'm unattractive. To: I'm grateful for eyes that see, legs that walk, lungs that breathe.
- From: I'm unlovable. To: When I was yet in my sin, God felt I was worth dying for.
- From: I'm unworthy. To: I'm grateful for the people who have never made me feel I have to earn their attention (name them).
- From: I'm unknown. To: God knows my name and orchestrates everything for my good.

I have reframed the toxic lie "I'm unwanted" to the truth that "I'm wanted by God." God created me and therefore God wants me. This is why I live my life to please him and him alone.

What lies do you need to reframe as truth so you can celebrate others and learn to see their success as your inspiration? Take a moment to think about this, and write down your "from" and "to" statements so you can build your own road map to a changed mindset.

Recall

Toxic comparison picks a fight where there is no prize.

When your insecurity is triggered, turn to the Holy Spirit and ask him for the power to reframe your thinking.

While toxic comparison emphasizes deficiency, God's truth emphasizes abundance.

A perceived lack is actually a disguised abundance.

Jonathan celebrated David because God celebrated David.

You kill comparison when you reframe it as celebration.

We can reframe abandonment as reassignment.

Greener grass is simply well-watered grass.

Heart problems can't be fixed in our heads.

Receive

I am not saying this because I am in need, for I have learned to be content whatever the circumstances. I know what it is to be in need, and I know what it is to have plenty. I have learned the secret of being content in any and every situation, whether well fed or hungry, whether living in plenty or in want. I can do all this through him who gives me strength. (Philippians 4:11–13)

Recite

Father, I need to replace toxic lies with your truth, so help me to see them for what they are and reframe them by what you say. May I receive your wisdom, guidance, hope, and conviction to change the thoughts I allow to occupy my mind. I surrender my mind to you and desire to make every thought captive in obedience to Christ. I am who you say I am, in Jesus's name!

Reflect

About five years ago, I broke fellowship with someone I once considered a close friend. They had been using me, and the pain of that recognition crushed me deeply. It took years and years of prayer, forgiveness, and self-work to heal. I had cut off all contact with them as part of that healing process, but they resurfaced last month and asked to meet and apologize for what happened. While 80 percent of me said no, I listened to the 20 percent that said yes because I was genuinely curious about what they had to say.

Within five minutes of talking, they begged for my forgiveness and explained how they never meant to hurt me. They explained how they had been dealing with traumatic events on their end and, because of it, didn't value our friendship the way they should have. I explained that I had forgiven them years ago to heal without being bitter, but they insisted that I say, "I forgive you," so I did. They let out a sigh of relief and changed the subject to more mundane things like family and careers.

Despite their asking me to be friends again, as the days passed, I never heard from them again. I questioned myself and asked, "What is it about me that made them disappear?" But God gave me a revelation that reframed that experience in a powerful, important way. God helped me see that sometimes we apologize to relieve guilt, not to restore relationship. My former friend didn't try to rectify the damage that was done because they were satisfied with simply knowing they were forgiven. Then God showed me . . . me.

God showed me how there have been times when I transgressed against him, then sought his forgiveness but not his fellowship. God shifted my focus away from my friend and back to me. Instead of feeling bitter toward my friend, I ended up feeling humbled and grateful for God's mercy. Reframing gives you the power to experience peace through gratitude.

Chapter Eleven

RELEASE IT

Hey, Nona! I'm hosting a gathering for Christian leaders and influencers and wanted to make sure you got an invite. Just click the link to see who's invited, and register if you can make it!"

I was pleasantly surprised by the text. It came right as God was writing this book through me. When I clicked the link and read the names listed, I was humbled and honored by the invitation. People I had admired from a distance across ministry, music, business, and more were on the list, along with several friends. But as I read down the list, I noticed something. *My name was missing.* Given the text, I had expected to see my name on the list, but that expectation was shattered, and I felt a familiar sensation bloom within me. As it was unfurling yet another petal of insecurity, the Holy Spirit said, "Practice what you preach." I knew *exactly* what he was saying.

It was a test.

I paused and took note of what I was feeling and thinking to recognize the emotion that was percolating in my heart. It was sadness. I felt dejected and disappointed. Then I took stock of what I was thinking: "See! I'm not good enough to make this list. I'm never good enough, no matter what I do. She has a global ministry with two million followers. He has multiple Grammys and sells out arenas. No wonder I'm not on the list. I'm nobody."

The comparison pity party was getting thick when I made the effort to focus my energy on reframing my thoughts: "I may not be on the list, but I'm on the host's heart. He reached out to me. And that's what matters most." As I allowed these thoughts to fill my mind, my emotions settled, and I felt the poison of comparison being neutralized in my heart. Next, I turned my attention to God with gratitude and said, "Lord, thank you for placing me on someone's heart and mind even when I'm not on the list. It is you, not a list, who opens doors. Thank you for your goodness!"

But that wasn't the end. I knew my reaction was an indication of insecurity, but I also knew that insecurity didn't have to be the boss of me. We become insecure when we secure our identity to insecure foundations. To be fully free from insecurity's power, I needed to detach my identity from whatever it was secured to that allowed toxic comparison to course through my heart.

I reflected on the question the Holy Spirit had asked me when I first felt grieved about being left out of the Full Blossom Conference: "Why does it matter?" It's such a simple question but also so profound. After I prayed and got honest with myself about the answer, I had to admit that I reacted because, in that moment, I had secured my identity to being on a list of important people. Because my name was missing, it triggered insecurity, which triggered toxic comparison.

When I looked at that list and didn't see my name, it hurt. But then the Holy Spirit asked me another question: "Who else is missing?" When I slowed down and read the list again, I noticed at least ten other names were missing. A few best-selling authors were missing, a few international speakers and prominent actors were missing, and a few award-winning music artists were missing too. It was then that I felt the Lord say, "This isn't an invitation to misery. It's an invitation to ministry."

Sensitivity to being left out gave me empathy for others who were left out. And when I reflected on it, I realized that being invited to the gathering wasn't about me. It was about putting me in a position to invite others who had been overlooked or forgotten. This revelation invigorated me. It energized me. It *inspired* me. So I contacted the host and asked if it would be okay for me to invite the people I didn't see listed, and he said, "Absolutely! Please do."

When I shared the link with the people who were missing from the list, several said, "Oh, wow! Thanks for thinking of me, but I'm not on the list. I don't think I'm supposed to be invited." I assured them that I had cleared it with the host and that they should *definitely* be there, to which they said, "Awesome! Count me in. Thanks for thinking of me." I felt more and more liberated with each invitation I sent because instead of continuing to feel overlooked, I instead felt empowered.

Releasing the expectation of recognition kills comparison in our hearts. By releasing myself from the expectation of being on that list and instead paving a way for others who also weren't listed, this test helped release me from the toxic power of comparison.

Jonathan released his expectation of wearing a crown that was destined for David. This allowed him to celebrate David's success without being threatened by what it would cost him.

John the Baptist released any expectation of personally leading the following he built—the following he built to follow Jesus. This allowed him to celebrate Jesus's ministry without feeling Jesus's success was his loss.

The apostle Paul released any expectation of personal glory by shutting down his fan club to promote unity in the church. This allowed him to celebrate the success of his co-laborers rather than drowning in toxic comparison when they built thriving churches that had more members than his did.

Freedom from insecurity requires releasing what we expected so we can lift others higher. And sometimes lifting others higher requires bending lower so they can stand on our shoulders.

Like that time your secret crush asked for your sister's phone number and you gave it so she could experience happiness, even at your expense.

Like that time you gave your coworker the speaking role for the team's big presentation, even though you put the deck together and giving the presentation was a role you wanted.

> Sometimes lifting others higher requires bending lower so they can stand on our shoulders.

Like that time you promoted your friend's new restaurant on your social media, even though you have your own restaurant to promote.

Lifting others higher is hard when we expect to be or want to be the one lifted higher. And it becomes almost impossible when the distance between where we are and where we want to be is filled with people we view as competition. Releasing expectations empowers us to build a bridge from insecurity to true freedom.

Check Your Expectations

Expectations are like a checklist that reminds us how close or far we are from where we think we should be. But the question we need to start asking ourselves is, *According to whom?* Before you say, "According to me," take a moment to really ask yourself this question because your honest answer might surprise you. I'll go first.

Five years ago I would have laughed if someone told me I would one day have more than five hundred Instagram followers. My first question would have been, "Why? Who would want to follow me? And for what?" It would have never occurred to me that tens of thousands of people would think I was worth listening to. If someone had told me then that I would sell thousands of books, I would have been awestruck and dumbfounded because I wouldn't have been able to wrap my mind around having a book in a store with my name on it.

As my professional and ministry circles expanded, I became aware that I was often the least known person in the room. I would be invited to speak at events with other speakers who had more than one hundred thousand followers on social media compared with my three hundred. I became acutely aware of how vast the chasm of influence was between me and them. That's when questions like "How do I get more followers?" drifted through my mind. What we are exposed to influences what we expect of ourselves, so the more prominent people I was exposed to, the more my expectations of myself shifted upward.

I was no longer satisfied with three hundred followers because the people I was associating with had more.

I remember the day my Instagram following hit one thousand like it was yesterday because it felt like a major milestone. As I traveled and spoke more, the number climbed slowly and steadily until I had around five thousand followers. That's when I decided to put some juice behind it by creating a sixty-second sermon clip and boosting it with a fifty-dollar ad for seven days. I was shocked when I had gained five hundred followers in a week, so I did it again and again until I was at almost seven thousand. At that point God convicted me and said, "Why are you looking for followers? Whose kingdom are you building? It doesn't matter how many followers *you* have if they aren't following *me* through you." Okay, Jesus. Edges snatched (I hear you, Lord).

Although I stopped the advertising campaign, I didn't release the expectation that I should have more followers. Why? Because I had secured my identity to the insecure foundation of social media affirmation. It was subtle and unintentional, but it happened. I expected to find worthiness on the other side of a larger following, so every new follower became a personal triumph and every unfollow a personal defeat. My sense of worthiness, which depended on the follow-count, likes, and comments, teetered precariously on a cliff.

And that is simply unsustainable.

By the time I found out I wasn't invited to speak at the Full Blossom Conference, I already knew I needed to make a change, but the process God has taken me through since then has taught me how to do it.

When our identity is secured to insecure foundations, it's so much easier to believe a toxic lie than a healthy truth. We seem to naturally gravitate toward the idea that we're not good enough for one reason or another, and the downward emotional and mental spiral that follows reinforces our unworthiness. This is why we have to recognize how we feel, what we think, and what we do when insecurity is triggered. This is why we have to reframe what we believe so that it aligns with God's truth. *And* this is why we need to ask ourselves the question the Holy Spirit asked me: Why does it matter?

If we answer honestly, this question uncovers the insecure foundations from which we need to release our identity so we can secure it instead to the firm foundation of who God says we are. Here are a few examples of what that might look like:

- Why does it matter that I wasn't elected to the PTA executive committee? Because I expected to find belonging on the other side.
- Why does it matter that my friend landed the music deal I've been working toward my entire life? Because I expected to find significance on the other side.
- Why does it matter that the book club didn't pick my book? Because I expected to have my intellect affirmed on the other side.
- Why does it matter that I didn't get the award? Because I expected to find worthiness on the other side.
- Why does it matter that the guy I met on Eharmony stopped responding to my texts? Because I expected to have my desirability affirmed on the other side.

Insecurity will make you believe that belonging, significance, affirmation, and worthiness reside somewhere outside of you. What if you can find belonging, significance, affirmation, and worthiness right where you are? Would you want to do that? I'm hoping your answer is a resounding yes!

Three Ways Forward

We often feel unfulfilled because we expect fulfillment on the other side of achievement, so when someone else gets it before or instead of us, our very identity hangs in the balance. But the incredible grace of God means we don't have to "arrive" before we can rest in who God created us to be. We can find that rest now when we choose to do three things: pray it forward, pay it forward, and power forward.

Pray It Forward

Many years ago I learned a prayer from a book that was sweeping the nation. A man named Jabez, whose name means "pain," prayed the prayer. He was given that name because of the severe pain his mother felt while birthing him (1 Chronicles 4:9). Despite his name, Jabez was more honorable than all his brothers.

The prayer of Jabez is simple but effective: "Jabez cried out to the God of Israel, 'Oh, that you would bless me and enlarge my territory! Let your hand be with me, and keep me from harm so that I will be free from pain.' And God granted his request" (1 Chronicles 4:10). Like many people, I started praying that prayer as a petition for God's grace and favor to rest on my life. As I have worked to release my identity from the insecure foundations that have made me feel like I don't measure up, this prayer has become an important part of my strategy.

When I see a post or hear through the grapevine that someone achieved something I wanted for myself and toxic emotions percolate in me, I pray the prayer of Jabez in earnest. But instead of praying it over my life, I pray it over theirs. Instead of asking God to bless me and enlarge my territory, I flip it: "Lord, I pray you would bless [name] and enlarge [her/his] territory! Let your hand be with [name], and keep [her/him] from harm so that [she/he] will be free from pain."

When I first started doing it, I felt a knot in my stomach as I asked God to bless them. They were already ahead of me in the achievement department, so asking God to bless them even more felt almost like asking him to keep me perpetually unfulfilled. At least that's how I felt. Instead, I found that the more I *prayed* for them, the less I *competed* with them. It's hard to compete with someone when you're praying for them to win. The stronger I gripped humility, the weaker I gripped pride. And as my grip on pride weakened, so did my grip on the expectation to be better than that individual.

> It's hard to compete with someone when you're praying for them to win.

The next time you feel threatened by another person's success, let the prayer of Jabez guide your heart, mind, and tongue to speak blessings over them in prayer. That's how you pray it forward.

Pay It Forward

Jesus said, "If anyone takes what belongs to you, do not demand it back. Do to others as you would have them do to you" (Luke 6:30–31). I have news for you. Just as you feel there is someone in this world you don't measure up to, there is most likely someone else in this world who feels they don't measure up to you. Although you may have no idea what I'm talking about and may even think, "I don't have enough for someone to use *me* as a measuring stick," just remember that you can have the lowliest of jobs and still have people say you think you're better than them because *they* think you're better than them. Insecurity isn't about what you have; it's about what your identity is secured to.

Sometimes the people who are fighting insecurity in themselves are the same ones who trigger insecurity in others. This is why I'm careful about what I post on social media. I don't post about what I have or who I'm with (unless it's my family) because I'm sensitive to how that can trigger toxic comparison in others. Instead, I try to keep my posts inspirational as a way to pay it forward. I want to use my insights about insecurity to help others.

You can do this in your life too. It's what I did when I invited people who were missing from the Christian influencer gathering invite list. I allowed the toxic comparison I felt to make me aware of others who weren't invited. I was able to use my awareness as a lever to help them.

- Instead of wallowing in jealousy of those who were elected to the PTA executive committee when you were not, ask the new committee how you can support them as a volunteer. Sign up to coordinate one of the committee's fundraisers. You can pay it forward.
- Instead of allowing bitterness to consume you when your friend gets the music deal you've been working for your entire life, ask them for social graphics you can use to promote their new album through your channels. You can pay it forward.

- Instead of succumbing to sadness and feeling snubbed when the book club doesn't pick your book, offer to host an upcoming book club meeting at your home so a discussion host doesn't have to plan the details. You can pay it forward.
- Instead of boycotting the awards dinner when you aren't nominated for the award, gather a group of friends and buy a table to show your support for the honorees. You can pay it forward.

Although you may initially struggle with the idea of volunteering for that PTA committee, posting about your friend's album, hosting a book club meeting, or attending that awards dinner, the very act of paying it forward in support of others will give you something even more valuable—the spiritual, emotional, and psychological payoff you need to move from insecurity to freedom. How do I know? Because that's what I've experienced and because that's what the Bible promises: "A generous person will prosper; whoever refreshes others will be refreshed" (Proverbs 11:25).

Power Forward

What's the source from which you derive your strength? Is it from the kind things people say about you? The number of followers you have? The degrees you have? How much money you have? All these sources of strength are insecure, which is why one unkind word can shake you. A few lost followers can shake you. Not being called "doctor" can shake you. A financial setback can shake you.

Getting free, truly free, from insecurity requires deriving your power from one source—the unchanging truth of God. The encouragement of the apostle Paul is to "be strong in the Lord and in his mighty power" (Ephesians 6:10). The Greek word translated "power" is *kratos*, which may also be rendered "dominion." The word envisions God's strength, power, and might that give us the ability to live lives donning the full armor of God (v. 11). When our insecurity is triggered and the toxin of comparison leaves us feeling frustrated, overwhelmed, or inadequate, instead of deriving substitute strength from other people's approval, we must train ourselves to derive our strength from the knowledge that, no matter what happens, God is sovereign and he is in control.

When you feel like you don't measure up and your life is less than what you wanted, you can rely on this promise:

> The LORD makes firm the steps
> > of the one who delights in him;
> though he may stumble, he will not fall,
> > for the LORD upholds him with his hand.
> (Psalm 37:23–24)

Your power does not reside outside of you; it resides in the fact that God orders your steps. Though you may experience failure, you are not a failure. Though you may experience disappointments, you are not a disappointment. Though you may experience mistakes, you are not a mistake.

Find Your Strength and Power

Many of us struggle with insecurity because we have secured our expectations to what we can do in our own power. Then we feel lacking when someone else achieves something we couldn't do in our own power. And yet God lacks nothing. A deficit mindset makes us believe what's possible ends with the limits of our capabilities because a deficit mindset believes there is a limited amount of good to go around. This is a lie. In God, there is not a limited supply of blessings. In God, there is not a limited supply of favor. In God, there is not a limited supply of grace. The key is to find our strength and power in the one whose strength and power is unlimited.

Pray it forward. Pay it forward. Power forward.

You can do this.

Recall

We become insecure when we secure our identity to insecure foundations.

Sensitivity to being left out gave me empathy for others who were left out.

Releasing the expectation of recognition kills comparison in our hearts.

Sometimes lifting others higher requires bending lower so they can stand on our shoulders.

What we are exposed to influences what we expect of ourselves.

It's hard to compete with someone when you are praying for them to win.

Sometimes the people who are fighting insecurity in themselves are the same ones who trigger insecurity in others.

A deficit mindset believes there is a limited amount of good to go around.

Receive

Humble yourselves before the Lord, and he will exalt you.
(James 4:10 ESV)

Recite

Father, help me to release the expectations I have been holding on to that have made me see myself as less than someone else. Help me to embrace your truth so I can pray for them and be genuinely happy for the good that comes their way. Give me eyes to see when others are struggling with insecurity so I can be a blessing and my experience becomes a ministry that glorifies you.

Reflect

Here's a detail I didn't share in the story of the Christian influencers gathering. After telling a couple of people about it when I didn't see their names on the invite list, they said, "Oh, yeah, I'm going." They hadn't reached out to ask me if I was going after not seeing my name on the list, so I started to feel some type of way about it. But then God reminded me that he was doing a work in *me*. I share this with you because as you begin to pray it forward and pay it forward, you may find that the people you are praying for and supporting don't reciprocate your efforts. And that's okay. Never forget that this work is for you, not them. Be encouraged.

Part Four

FINAL THOUGHTS

Chapter Twelve

LIVE ENCOURAGED AND INSPIRED

It's so good to see you again," I said as my friend sat down beside me to get her makeup done. We were in a television studio in Nashville, Tennessee, to film a week of conversations for TBN's *Better Together* show.

"You too! How are you? How's the family?" she asked as our makeup artists started prepping our faces.

"Everyone is doing great," I said. "I'm working on my third book, so staying busy."

"Oh, really? What's it about?" she asked.

"Well, the working title is *Killing Comparison*, and my goal is to use my own struggle to get free from insecurity to help readers. The main idea is that insecurity results from securing our identity to an insecure foundation—such as what we have, who we know, what we do. But when we scroll through Instagram and see others doing better than we are in that area, toxic comparison triggers insecurity."

"Nona, I am so glad you're writing about that! Listen, I've had books on the *New York Times* bestseller list, I've preached in more than two hundred countries, and I have a million followers on Instagram. But a few years ago a list was published of the top women in ministry, and I wasn't on the list. It crushed me, I mean, it *devastated* me!"

I was surprised to know that even at her level something like that devastated her. I imagined her success would have shielded her from that type of pain, but no.

She continued, "I called a friend who was on the list and told her I wasn't on it, and the first thing she said was, 'Am I on the list?' When I told her she was, she breathed a sigh of relief. This book is so necessary."

It was amazing to me that she could relate to the message of this book because she is someone whose books have been a source of inspiration to me through the years. And yet here she was. Struggling just like me. And that's why this last chapter is so important. You see, if you read this book and thought, "Wow, it's so awesome that Nona is free from insecurity. I hope I get free someday too," I need you to know that my freedom is won daily, hour by hour, as my identity is assaulted by images, words, and actions that lead me to question my worth. Don't believe me? Let me share a few examples from the past month.

- I was uninvited from speaking at a major conference. I've had entire events canceled or postponed, but I've never been uninvited. The reason? The host decided to use my speaking slot for something else. Interestingly, when the organization first reached out to my team, I agreed to do the event for less than half my typical honorarium due to their budget constraints. My team never mentioned that to them, but when it came down to it, my spot was expendable. *I* was expendable.

- One of my son's teachers sent me an email saying he had been tardy multiple times, and if he was tardy two more times, he would be expelled from school. His tardiness was a combination of being dropped off late and getting to class late on his own. As I rolled onto campus for pickup that day and noticed the many smiling moms and their smiling children, I was lost in thought. "What would it look like if my son was expelled from this school when I'm the one preaching and teaching about leadership across the country?" The tone of the conversation I had with my son that evening was laced more with fear of what people would say about me than it was with understanding why he was tardy.

- A person I have long admired in ministry offered to let me spend a weekend with her. I decided to take her up on the offer because I found myself in a bit of a funk. I texted her to set up the visit, but after she asked me when I could come and I asked for a few dates that would work for her, she went silent. I waited to hear back for a couple of days, but when she didn't respond, the cascade of toxic thoughts began to fall. "Why did you think she was serious, Nona? She was just humoring you when she made that offer. You're nowhere near her level, so why would she make time for you?"

Over the last month I've had to contend with insecurity in my ministry, my mothering, and my friendships, and you know what? Tomorrow is a new day that will challenge me in new ways. The reason I wrote this book is because I wanted to give you the toolbox I now use to meet each of these challenging moments with power. Not *my* power. *God's* power. The power to live encouraged and inspired.

Befriend Yourself

The word *encourage* has two components: the prefix *en-* and the word *courage*. The prefix *en-* means "within or in," and *courage* means "strength in the face of pain or grief."[9] When we put the two together, we get *encourage*, which is to instill strength within someone who is facing pain or grief.

When your newly minted sixth grader dreads his first day of middle school because he thinks he won't make any friends, you instill strength within him by reminding him of the new friends he'll make every year and that the best friends he already has will be in his classes again.

When your neighbor tells you her husband's colonoscopy gave the doctor cause for concern, you take one look at the fear in her eyes and instill strength by grabbing her hand, squeezing it tight, and offering to pray with her.

When you find out your college roommate has suffered a miscarriage, you pick up the phone and call her to listen to her cries of grief. Then you instill strength within her by sharing your own story of finding peace after miscarriage and letting her know you won't let her walk through her grief alone.

When we encourage someone, we place courage *in* them. We don't do this by simply patting them on the back and saying, "There, there, it'll be okay." We do it by giving them something to place their hope in.

Many of us do a great job of encouraging others, but when it comes to our own pain, we tend to do the opposite. Instead of placing our hope in God, we look for and cling to any evidence that supports the toxic lie that we're broken, defective, or less-than. And the worst part of it all is that we do it by default, without even trying. But do you know what the opposite of courage is? It's fear. When we become fearful, chances are good that we are running low on courage, so we have to develop a muscle for encouraging *ourselves* as much as we would encourage anyone else who felt the way we do. One of the ways we build this muscle is by treating ourselves like a friend. Here's what that looks like:

> When we encourage someone, we place courage *in* them.

If a friend told me she was feeling sad because she had been uninvited to speak at an event, I would pull her into a loving embrace and let her know it wasn't her fault. Whether or not she admitted it, I would know that's what she believed. I would remind her that God was at work in her life, orchestrating every closed door as well as every open one. I would help her reflect on how many times the closed doors were strategic redirections that led her to something better. And I would invite her to place her hope in the character of God—a God who loves her more than she could ever imagine. I would say all this to her to instill courage in her in the face of her pain.

If a friend told me her son's risk of expulsion made her feel like a failure of a mom, I would take her hand while assuring her that she is a great mother. I would encourage her to remember that her job is to teach her children how to live a life that honors God and that she could use the tardiness warning as an opportunity to teach consequences. I would help her focus her energy on the ministry of motherhood, a ministry that comes with incredible highs and incredible lows and remind her that her unyielding love for her children through it all is a gift they will soon appreciate. I would invite her to place her hope in the truth of God's Word, that if she does her part to train up her children in the way they should go, they will not depart from it when they are old (Proverbs 22:6).

If a friend came to me and told me she felt like she wasn't good enough because another friend hadn't responded to her texts, I would nod knowingly and affirm a feeling I know all too well. I would soothe her anxiety by reminding her that a nonresponse is often a symptom of distraction more than rejection. Since the friend had always been loving and welcoming under other circumstances, it was entirely possible she simply got distracted, not that she didn't want to spend time together. We would laugh about times we too had responded to texts mentally but not in reality, only to remember weeks later and have to apologize for our delayed response. I would invite her to place her hope in what she knows to be true of her friend so she could reject the toxic lies seeking to drown her in insecurity.

Perhaps you affirm your friends in similar ways, so what if you did it for yourself as well? Instead of succumbing to sadness or fear or bitterness, what if you gave yourself a courage infusion? Speak words of encouragement when you feel depleted, anxious, worthless, and hopeless. All it requires is allowing yourself to believe the best, even when the worst seems most probable.

When Indra is named the new team leader instead of you, you can encourage yourself by meeting with the person who appointed her and getting feedback on how to position yourself for a promotion next time. You can enlist their support through periodic check-ins to discuss your performance and how to get more recognition for your contributions. Instead of succumbing to discouragement and bitterness, you can choose to walk in God's power, the power that gives courage.

When the other women in your weight-loss club hit their goal weights but you hover at a loss of three pounds after months of dieting and exercising, you can encourage yourself by letting their success remind you of what's possible. Let their success keep you committed to the process. Instead of succumbing to discouragement and guilt, you can choose to walk in God's power, the power that gives courage.

When our insecurity goes unchecked, it causes us to stop trying. Stop dreaming. Stop hoping. Toxic insecurity makes us believe there is no point because we'll never be good enough or measure up to the expectations of others. It's in those moments—the moments when we aren't sure we want to even keep trying—that we need to couple encouragement with inspiration.

Three Sources of Inspiration

While encouragement gives us strength in the face of pain or grief, the reality for many of us is that encouragement can only take us so far. When our pain is deeper than the depths of the ocean and when our grief feels like a black hole, placing our hope in the goodness of God's character can require an act of God on its own.

I once met a beautiful, effervescent podcast host who invited me to talk about my book *Success from the Inside Out*. Our conversation was going wonderfully when she asked me how I was able to forgive my mom and her boyfriend for what they did to me when I was a child. I explained that I had learned to place my hope in God and to trust that he could make something good come out of the bad that happened. She grew quiet, and what she said next made my heart drop.

"But how do you place your hope in God when there is no hope?" she asked. "My son, who is brilliant and full of life, is dying of cancer. He's in college. Loves God. Is kind and generous and gracious. And God is taking him from me. How can God make something good out of this?"

> When the weight of life makes it hard to breathe, we don't need affirmations, we need oxygen.

My mother's heart responded with tears. Before I could even think about a response, her grief met my heart and we simply paused in the moment. Sure, I could have offered her Scriptures on hope, and I could even have told her about giving birth at twenty weeks and having to watch my baby boy Daniel die, but I didn't. I didn't do any of that because I know that when the weight of life makes it hard to breathe, we don't need affirmations, we need oxygen.

Instead of offering her Scriptures, I offered her myself. We exchanged cell numbers, and I prayed for her and her family in earnest. When she shared the tragic news of her son's passing, I let a couple of months go by before I called her and spent an hour simply opening my heart wide to receive her pain. I encouraged her by affirming that her grief wasn't an anomaly nor was it a lack of faith (as some people had told her). I prayed a blessing over her that God would make his presence known in the darkness of her grief. And in response she simply said, "Nona, thank you for making the time to be with me. It gives me hope. And I have so little of that right now."

I mentioned in an earlier chapter that to "inspire" is to breathe oxygen into your lungs. Inspiration is the process of taking in that which gives life. That which gives hope. That which gives purpose. That which gives joy. When it's difficult to find hope, purpose, or joy in our circumstances, we need to actively seek out inspiration, that which can restore life and energy to our souls. And when others are challenged, we need to extend inspiration to them as well.

How do we do that? Here are three sources of inspiration I turn to when I need hope, purpose, and joy—the Bible, social media, and friendships.

The Bible

I find it entertaining to read secular self-help books. They usually purport to have some groundbreaking, never-before-heard-of insight to help you find peace, but their revolutionary idea is often simply a two-hundred-page repackaging of biblical truths from Proverbs, the Psalms, a parable, or a Pauline epistle.

For example, one of my favorite self-help books is *Essentialism* by Greg McKeown. I use it as a resource for my leadership academy. Its central thesis is that before you take on something new, you need to consider whether you have the capacity to do it. This is a concept Jesus taught with a parable two thousand years ago.

> Suppose one of you wants to build a tower. Won't you first sit down and estimate the cost to see if you have enough money to complete it? For if you lay the foundation and are not able to finish it, everyone who sees it will ridicule you, saying, "This person began to build and wasn't able to finish."
>
> Or suppose a king is about to go to war against another king. Won't he first sit down and consider whether he is able with ten thousand men to oppose the one coming against him with twenty thousand? If he is not able, he will send a delegation while the other is still a long way off and will ask for terms of peace. (Luke 14:28–32)

After more than two decades of walking with Jesus, I have found the unchanging truth of God's Word to be as inspiring to me today as it has been to others for centuries. For me, biblical inspiration isn't only about memorizing Scripture. Biblical inspiration allows Scripture to speak into my situation in relevant ways. For example, when I launched my Facebook Live talk show and podcast, I was so excited about it, I never stopped to estimate its cost—what it might require of me. I never considered how I would fit the work required to do it well into an already overflowing schedule. But you know why I plowed ahead and did it anyway? Because others did. Friends were launching podcasts left and right, especially since this was near the start of the pandemic lockdown and they suddenly had a lot of time on their hands. But I didn't suddenly have more time. Rather, my available time became even more limited as every church on earth suddenly needed the support of me and my team at Facebook.

As I reflected on Luke 14, I felt a sense of peace come over me because it inspired me to count the cost. And when I started counting, it quickly added up to a cost I simply couldn't pay. Although it dismayed the team I had gathered to produce it, I shut down the podcast. It was painful for sure, but necessary. Applying the wisdom of this Scripture has allowed me to experience the joy of my purpose by ensuring my time is spent where God has graced me.

Social Media

This may come as a surprise to you since I have been forthcoming about how what I've seen on social media has triggered struggles with toxic comparison, but here's the thing. Although social media is getting an increasingly bad rap from users and researchers alike, I have found that curating my social feed to follow only people who inspire me is an easy solution. The people who walk away from social media feeling worse about themselves are usually following people who *expire* them, so I make it a point not to follow those types of accounts.

I don't follow political pundits, socialites, or anyone who posts only about how glamorous their life is. Political pundits and elected officials know that their messages go far and wide when they are doused in anger, hostility, and degradation, so why would I, as someone who loves God and wants to follow the command to love others, keep that kind of content constantly in my line of sight? I don't want to be angry. I don't want to see my fellow image-bearers as idiots and morons. And, frankly, I don't want to take delight in another person's demise.

The psalmist says,

> Blessed is the one
> who does not walk in step with the wicked

> or stand in the way that sinners take
>
> or sit in the company of mockers. (Psalm 1:1)

If you are connected with anyone who uses the name of Jesus in ungodly ways, unfollow them. If any professing Christian you are following is indistinguishable from the unsaved, unfollow them. If anyone you are following posts a Scripture verse one minute, then posts a meme degrading someone the next, unfollow them. Follow people who use their platform to encourage and inspire. People who give you ideas for how to get from where you are to where you want to be by showing you their own journey—transparently. The good and the bad. The successes and the failures.

> Follow people who use their platform to encourage and inspire.

On the practical side, if you have a Facebook profile, you can visit a friend's profile and choose to unfollow *or* unfriend. The difference is that when you unfollow, you remain friends but no longer see what they post. It's a great option if unfriending would cause real-life drama. On Instagram, you have the option of unfollowing or muting a person's posts. If you mute posts, you will no longer see their posts, and if you unfollow them, you will no longer be connected with the person. Either way, these actions can help you weed your feed of the people and content that falls short of making you a better person.

Friendships

Living inspired requires guarding our hearts like they're the Federal Reserve. Sometimes we keep people in our lives who trigger sadness, fear, bitterness, guilt, and more, simply because we don't want to disappoint people. We stay in jobs that leave us drained. We hang on to relationships that leave us exhausted. We volunteer for projects that leave us irritated. But living inspired requires cleaning out our purpose pantry—actively inspecting the relationships and situations to which we are connected and identifying any that have expired or no longer serve a purpose in our lives.

This decluttering is one of the more difficult aspects of living an inspired life. Some of us have wrapped our identity around relationships that drain the life out of us.

Maybe your best friend constantly bashes the side hustle you're trying to build into a business.

Maybe your boyfriend pushes you to compromise your integrity even though he knows you're waiting for marriage to have sex.

Maybe the colleague you consider a close friend regularly asks to borrow one hundred dollars until payday, but payday comes and he appears to suffer repayment amnesia.

All of these are examples of relationships that have expired or no longer serve a purpose—and it's time to let them go. Jesus said, "[My Father] cuts off every branch in me that bears no fruit, while every branch that does bear fruit he prunes so that it will be even more fruitful" (John 15:2). I'm going to repeat this so you can read it again. Jesus said, "[My Father] *cuts off* every branch in me that bears no fruit, while every branch that does bear fruit he prunes so that it will be even more fruitful" (emphasis added).

Have you ever cut off or pruned a branch? I have. The interesting thing is that you use the same tool to accomplish both jobs. And a similar principle applies to friendships. Some friendships must be cut off to help you live inspired, while others have to be pruned by setting boundaries. Whether they're cut off completely or pruned, there will be pain. But healthy, fruitful friendships are a vital part of living inspired because the people who have access to your heart also shape your thoughts. To protect your heart from discouragement and expiration, ensure that your friendships are healthy.

On the other side of a healthy heart is the ability to lead others to freedom.

Leading Others to Freedom

I love this quote that is attributed to Harriet Tubman but may very well be made up: "I freed a thousand slaves and could have freed more if only they knew they were slaves."

When I reflect on my journey to stay free from insecurity and the toxic comparison it creates, one thing stands out: the area of my deepest bondage is always the area of my deepest denial. Often we think if we simply reject the idea that we are insecure, we will reject insecurity too, but we won't be healed from the sickness we ignore. We can only be healed from the sickness we confront. And this is where I want to issue a challenge.

My hope and prayer is that this book has not only brought you face-to-face with the toxic lies that have caused you to secure your identity to insecure foundations but also made you aware of how the words you speak and actions you take can create insecurity in others. *That ends today*. Today, I deputize you to lead others to the freedom you are winning for yourself. When someone else begins to declare they aren't good enough, instead of saying, "Yes you are," and patting them on the back as usual, commit yourself to helping them do the work to get free.

- Buy them a copy of this book and encourage them to read a chapter a day.
- Text them each morning as an accountability check-in, and ask them what they learned about themselves from the chapter they read the night before.
- Set time once a week to sit down together and talk in depth about what they're discovering about themselves.
- Do the work together by talking through the three questions from chapter 6: What do I focus on that triggers insecurity? What do I choose to believe when my insecurity is triggered? What do I do in response to what I believe? Then do the recognize, reframe, and release work from chapters 8 through 11 so they can feel supported during their personal discovery.
- Ask them how you can partner with them in the future to help them live encouraged and inspired.

Often the people who struggle with insecurity are the ones we least expect. Instead of assuming someone doesn't need your encouragement, give it. Instead of assuming they don't need your support, give it. Instead of assuming they don't need your compassion, give it.

I am deputizing you not only to kill comparison in yourself but also to help kill comparison in others. Take off the mental boxing gloves and running shoes because neither the fight nor the race is against them. The only opponent we need to defeat is the opponent within us. Although getting free from insecurity sometimes feels like shadowboxing with an invisible adversary, I have discovered that not all shadows are bad. The psalmist wrote, "Whoever dwells in the shelter of the Most

High will *rest* in the *shadow* of the Almighty" (Psalm 91:1, emphasis added).

When you feel unprotected, unworthy, inadequate, unwanted, or unloved, you can find rest in the place where worthiness has always been. Not on Instagram or in the gym. Not chairing a committee or getting matches on Tinder. Not at an award show or on a conference stage. You can find rest in the shadow of God's protection from human rejection by securing your identity to who he says you are. You were created worthy.

Recall

Tomorrow is a new day that will challenge us in new ways.

When we encourage someone, we place courage *in* them.

Biblical inspiration allows Scripture to speak into our situations in relevant ways.

Follow people who use their platform to encourage and inspire.

Some of us have wrapped our identity around relationships that drain the life out of us.

People who have access to your heart also shape your thoughts.

The area of deepest bondage is always the area of deepest denial.

We can only be healed from the sickness we confront.

Receive

Carry each other's burdens, and in this way you will fulfill the law of Christ. If anyone thinks they are something when they are not, they deceive themselves. (Galatians 6:2–3)

Recite

Father, as I commit my heart and mind to focus on what gives me courage and inspiration, lead me to remember others who also need courage and inspiration. Help me to be sensitive to the hurts that create insecurity in others so that I can become a source of healing and hope in their lives.

Reflect

This book has been difficult to write because it required me to share what I would much rather hide beneath a confidence costume. But what's the point of hiding if my experience can lead to someone's healing? This is the mindset I've had during each chapter. Each story. Each insight that has required my transparency. I invite you to join me in crucifying pride so that we can kill what is killing us. I have chosen to push beyond my fear because your freedom is worth it. And so is the freedom of everyone who will be inspired by your victory over toxic comparison.

AFTERWORD

As our journey together comes to a close, I pray you feel free and inspired. I pray you feel empowered and encouraged. I pray you feel uplifted and equipped. But as those warm and fuzzy feelings wrap themselves around you like a friendly hug, I need you to know they won't last forever.

Tomorrow, this weekend, next week, or a few weeks from now, something will trigger an old familiar sensation within you that you can now name as toxic comparison. Something will reveal that an insecure foundation is still present in your life.

Your little sister will graduate with her master's degree, while you spend another year saving to go back to college.

A fellow Bible teacher at your church will be invited to speak at your church's big annual event instead of you.

Your sweet, pretty cousin will be the center of attention at the family dinner—*again*.

Someone you follow on social media will announce yet *another* incredible opportunity they've had that you wanted.

When you see these posts, you will be tempted to spiral into the familiar patterns of toxic comparison. But instead of succumbing, whisper four words to yourself: "Why does it matter?"

You can employ the frameworks shared in this book to take control of your feelings, thoughts, and actions. And when all is said and done, you can flash a grin to no one in particular because you will know you've won.

You will know that, when the toxin of comparison tried to seep in and kill your sense of worth and identity, you stood your ground and said, "Not today!" When the toxin of comparison tried to make you see another person as your competition, you chose to celebrate them instead. And when the toxin of comparison tried to make you believe you don't measure up, the truth of God's Word will remind you that, even if you don't have what they have, you have the only thing that matters—an identity grounded in the truth of who God says you are.

Even if no one ever applauds you or compliments you or supports you, when it comes to the purpose God has placed in you, I hope you are as confident as Jonathan when he said, "Nothing can hinder the LORD from saving, whether by many or by few" (1 Samuel 14:6). You are worthy. You are approved. And no one can do what you do. You were born an original, and God doesn't intend for you to die a duplicate. The world needs everything you have to offer—without comparison.

ACKNOWLEDGMENTS

Transparent moment: After writing this book and several others, can you believe that words escape me to accurately describe just how thankful I am to have this book in the world? Words like *thankful* and *grateful* feel hollow compared with what I actually feel, because this book represents the tangible culmination of my journey to victory over comparison-born insecurity.

I've had countless experiences while writing this book that would have normally triggered a toxic spiral of self-loathing. Instead, they simply triggered awareness of how far God has brought me. Because of this, I want to first express my deepest appreciation, gratitude, and devotion to the Holy Spirit for leading me into unknown terrain so that I could emerge out of the darkness with a road map to victory for people like you and me.

The fact is that I would be unable to share this road map with you had it not been for the wonderful team at Zondervan who believed in my vision for this book and came alongside me to ensure it is shared with the world. First, to Webster Younce, thank you for being quick to see the potential in this message. I thought it would take months of review and discussion before moving forward, but a few weeks after receiving my proposal, you said, "Let's do it!" That was such an encouragement to me. Carolyn McCready, thank you for your encouragement and enthusiasm as you edited my book. Your suggestions and ideas were thoughtful and considerate and helped make sure my thinking was as clear as possible. Kim Tanner, having your eyes on my final edited manuscript was such a gift! You know my voice so well after editing other works of mine, and the way you fine-tune a story is simply magic. I am also deeply grateful to the incredible Zondervan marketing team who enthusiastically embraced this message and have worked with utmost passion and professionalism to get this message out: Paul Fisher, Katie Painter, Sarah Falter, and Matt Bray.

To the one and only Margot Starbuck, thank you for being such a joy to work with as you pushed me to deeper depths and higher heights in the writing of my draft manuscript. Your questions, pushback, affirmation, and ideas polished this book until it shone. You not only understood my voice, but you understood the reader's heart. You found a way to help me connect the two when they were even the slightest bit misaligned, and that means everything to me.

Thank you to Lysa TerKeurst and the entire Compel team for helping me construct a solid foundation on which to build my story. The training is a priceless gift for authors, and I left feeling inspired, motivated and equipped to write this book.

In this same vein, I am deeply grateful to my one-hundred-plus member book squad. Each of you lovingly gave of your time and energy to help make this book resonate. We laughed together, cried together, learned together, and exhaled together as your feedback shaped this into something truly special. The manuscript I started with and the book people now read are two completely different works, thanks to you!

To my chief of staff, Antwan Steele, thank you for being the maestro orchestrator of my life. Your work helped me create the capacity needed so none of the many balls I juggle across my various roles and responsibilities would drop while writing this. You also project managed my book squad focus group and made certain all feedback was synthesized so I could act on it.

Thank you to Eliana Caceres, who volunteered to facilitate the book squad discussions and gather feedback from members every couple of weeks for months. I am so grateful for your friendship and your willingness to serve.

Thank you to my amazing social media manager, Chris Britt, who has been instrumental in supporting this book launch and being the creative genius of my team.

To my husband, Tim, thank you for being the most consistent source of affirmation in my life. You see me at my best (speaking in front of thousands) and at my worst (wearing a hair bonnet and sweats), but your look of adoration is the same in both contexts. You are my covering, not my lid. Thank you for everything you are to me and my forever babies, TJ and Isaac.

To my many friends and supporters who purchased this book before it was even released, I cannot thank you enough for your faith in me. You have no idea how much your gesture kept me going as we made our way to this day. You didn't have to do it, but you did. And I am grateful to all of you.

NOTES

1. Edgar Degas in Joseph Demakis, comp., *The Ultimate Book of Quotations* (Raleigh: Lulu Enterprises, 2012), 20.
2. Nathan Rutstein, *Healing Racism in America: A Prescription for the Disease* (Springfield, MA: Whitcomb, 1993), 99.
3. Australian Institute of Professional Counselors, "The Rise and Rise of the Selfie," *Counselling Connection*, September 17, 2019, https://www.counsellingconnection.com/index.php/2019/09/17/the-rise-and-rise-of-the-selfie/.
4. Craig Groeschel, *Winning the War in Your Mind: Change Your Thinking, Change Your Life* (Grand Rapids: Zondervan, 2021), 16.
5. Asha Z. Ivey-Stephenson et al., "Suicidal Ideation and Behaviors among High School Students—Youth Risk Behavior Survey, United States, 2019," *Morbidity and Mortality Weekly Report Supplement* 69, no. 1 (August 21, 2020): 47–55, https://doi.org/10.15585/mmwr.su6901a6.
6. *Merriam-Webster*, s.v. "focus (*n*.)," accessed February 28, 2022, https://www.merriam-webster.com/dictionary/focus.
7. Brian Odegaard and Ladan Shams, "The Brain's Tendency to Bind Audiovisual Signals Is Stable but Not General," *Psychological Science* 27, no. 4 (April 2016): 583–91, https://doi.org/10.1177/0956797616628860.
8. "Depression," World Health Organization, September 13, 2021, https://www.who.int/news-room/fact-sheets/detail/depression.
9. *Merriam-Webster*, s.v. "courage (*n*.)," accessed March 29, 2022, https://www.merriam-webster.com/dictionary/courage; *Merriam-Webster*, s.v. "en-," accessed March 29, 2022, https://www.merriam-webster.com/dictionary/en.

Success from the Inside Out

Power to Rise from the Past to a Fulfilling Future

Nona Jones

Join corporate executive and leadership speaker
Nona Jones as she takes you on a personal journey
of healing from the past so you can move forward with freedom and hope.

Many of us aspire to achieve status, wealth, and notability in the hopes that those things will erase the pain of our past. But for those who have experienced trauma, like Nona Jones, success requires more than a changed mindset—it requires repairing a broken spirit.

Success from the Inside Out charts the course of Nona's breakthrough—a course that can also lead you out of the storms of your past or present. Through her own remarkable story and insights, Nona helps you:

- Claim victory at the place where the defeat happened
- Recognize ways you use work to cover up inward brokenness
- Still the voices in your head that say you aren't good enough
- Choose fulfilling success instead of empty success
- Map your mile-markers toward your biggest goals
- Push through brokenness into a breakthrough

"Nona Jones's transparency and insight into her most painful experiences will undoubtedly help readers overcome their darkest experiences so they can experience all the goodness and success that is waiting for them on the path to redemption and empowerment!"

—Laila Ali, author, TV host, champion boxer, and CEO

"In Success from the Inside Out, Nona Jones shows us that God's grace is strong enough to lift us up when we have no strength left with which to stand. This book is for anyone who needs freedom from their past to fully embrace their future."

—Bishop T. D. Jakes, *New York Times* bestselling author
and senior pastor of the Potter's House of Dallas

Available in stores and online!

From Social Media to Social Ministry

A Guide to Digital Discipleship

Nona Jones

This book outlines digital discipleship principles for building an online community and provides practical instruction for how to do it no matter how big or small a local church may be.

Although social technology has been around for more than two decades, church leaders have long bristled at the idea of church online, ranking it as the last concern on their minds in Barna's 2020 state of the church report published February 3, 2020. And then, three weeks later, COVID-19 closed the doors of every church on earth and suddenly forced them entirely online.

Nona Jones, a globally acclaimed thought leader on leveraging technology for ministry, had been leading a movement and sounding the alarm for several years to make digital discipleship a central part of every church's ministry approach. In *From Social Media to Social Ministry*, she outlines her digital discipleship principles and provides practical instruction for how to do it no matter how big or small a local church may be. There are plenty of books to help churches build a social media strategy, but this is the first book of its kind that goes beyond digital marketing to digital ministry.

Readers will leave this book with:

- Clarity on what discipleship truly is
- The data that underscores the urgency for digital discipleship
- Understanding of the resources required to do it well
- A step-by-step guide on how to implement digital discipleship into ministry plans
- Knowledge of the differences among and purposes of the most popular social platforms, as well as the tools best positioned for digital ministry

Available in stores and online!